From Vietnam to Hell

From Vietnam
to Hell

Interviews with Victims
of Post-Traumatic Stress Disorder

Shirley Dicks

McFarland & Company, Inc., Publishers

Jefferson, North Carolina, and London

i

The present work is a reprint of the softcover edition of From Vietnam to Hell: Interviews with Victims of Post-Traumatic Stress Disorder, first published in 1990 by McFarland.

LIBRARY OF CONGRESS CATALOGUING-IN-PUBLICATION DATA

Dicks, Shirley, 1940–
    From Vietnam to hell : interviews with victims of post-traumatic stress disorder / by Shirley Dicks.
        p.   cm.
    Includes index.

    ISBN 978-0-7864-6944-4
    softcover : acid free paper ∞

    1. Post-traumatic stress disorder — Patients — Interviews.
    2. Vietnamese Conflict, 1961–1975 — Veterans — United States — Interviews.   I. Title.
    RC552.P67D52 2012
    616.85' 212 — dc20   89-43647

BRITISH LIBRARY CATALOGUING DATA ARE AVAILABLE

Front cover design by David K. Landis (Shake It Loose Graphics)

Manufactured in the United States of America

McFarland & Company, Inc., Publishers
    Box 611, Jefferson, North Carolina 28640
    www.mcfarlandpub.com

This book is dedicated
to my ex-husband Nelson
who served in Vietnam in the Marine Corps
and for Dick
who has been so patient
while I sat at my computer day after day,
never complaining,
well hardly ever.

Table of Contents

Introduction

For many Americans the Vietnam War is over and long forgotten, but for thousands of veterans they still live the horror of this war. In flashbacks, nightmares and other symptoms, they relive the time they spent in the jungle. Some turn to alcohol, others to drugs, to blot the inner agony that has no name, but many faces. Some mistreat their wives and children; some withdraw from society altogether.

This book tells the stories of some of these Vietnam veterans who have been to hell and back, and the wives who stood by their men. The stories are heartbreaking and meant to inform people about post-traumatic stress disorder. Some of these men are on death row. They were taught to kill women and children; they were taught that life wasn't important; then they were never debriefed once back home. One day they were in the jungles of Vietnam; the next they were back in the States.

All the stories are true. I began by interviewing death row inmates. One of the men gave me the name of Chuck Dean of Point Man Ministries in the State of Washington. He put me in touch with many others who suffered from PTSD. I decided to tell their stories because my ex-husband suffered from this disorder. He refused to get help, and I began to realize that thousands of veterans felt the same way about going for help. By reading the stories of others who have been able to change their lives, they might decided to seek the help that they also need.

All names are real, although six wanted only their first names used. All the interviews were done by phone and were tape recorded. I thank each and every one who willingly told his or her story.

Post-Traumatic Stress Disorder

The essential feature of post-traumatic stress disorder is the development of characteristic symptoms following a psychologically distressing event outside the range of usual human experience. It is usually experienced with intense fear and helplessness. The traumatic event can be reexperienced in a variety of ways with the most common of them being recurrent dreams during which the event is reexperieced. In rare instances there are dissociative states lasting from a few seconds to several hours, or even days, during which they relive the event.

Vietnam veterans often have intrusive thoughts and flashbacks triggered by common experiences such as popcorn popping and the smell of diesel fuel.

Vietnam veterans often have few friends. Many isolate themselves from their family both emotionally and geographically. They begin to fantasize about moving away from their problems. They often believe that no one understands or cares.

The Vietnam veteran who is experiencing PTSD is cold, aloof, uncaring, and has a constant fear of "losing control." He often feels a sense of helplessness, worthlessness and dejection.

The prevalence of PTSD and other postwar psychological problems is significantly higher among those with high levels of exposure to combat and other war zone stressors in Vietnam.

About 40 percent of Vietnam veterans have been divorced at least once. PTSD has a substantial negative impact not only on a veteran's own life, but also on the lives of those who are close to him. They tend to have more marital and family problems than do Vietnam veterans without PTSD. They report more marital and relational problems, more problems related to parenting, and substantially poorer family adjustment than those without the disorder. Their spouses report being less happy and satisfied with their lives and having more general psychological distress than do the

Post-Traumatic Stress Disorder

spouses of veterans without PTSD. Their children tend to have more behavioral problems.

The National Vietnam Veterans findings indicate that Vietnam veterans with PTSD lead profoundly disrupted lives. The relationship between PTSD and the development of other adjustment problems has not been thoroughly explored.

Post-traumatic stress disorder (also called delayed stress reaction) is not a disease; it is a reaction to the extreme stress endured during and after the war in Southeast Asia. The major responses to PTSD are depression, anger, anxiety, sleep disturbances, psychic or emotional numbing, emotional constriction, loss of interest in work and activities, and a tendency to react to stress by using survival tactics.

During the course of their lives, more than half of Vietnam veterans will have PTSD. Thousands of those vets will be put in prisons and many more will commit suicide. The substance abuse wards are full. Few people can understand the pain, loneliness, and stress Vietnam veterans have undergone since serving their country.

Dale Barnes

U.S. Army

"I originally went into the Air Force but decided I wanted to be in the Army. I was able to cross over and was assigned to the Special Forces, spending a total of two and a half years in Vietnam, a year of that doing hospital time.

"I operated with what they called Hatchet and Snatch teams. My job was primarily intelligence, gathering and destruction. I tried to break up intelligent networks with the Viet Cong.

"In 1968, I was with a snatch mission to get back some of our POWs that were in the process of being transferred. We were successful and also rescued five French prisoners. The process of that mission was very costly, however. I lost 11 men to free the seven men that I freed.

"We'd run operations in which I'd go in with my team and we would identify particular intelligence networks, trace them down and eliminate them. That was my job, and I did it. I think we were successful even though we lost a lot of men. I was much younger and more physically fit for jungle fighting. We, for some reason, thought we were invincible and that the bullets wouldn't hurt us. I was shot five times which proved that theory wrong.

"There was a village, I can't recall the name of it right now, just across the Laotian border. My team was to go in and transport back to one of our bases, into Vietnam, an important person that was located in the camp. But a klick [one kilometer] from the village, we heard a lot of gunfire. We hurried into the village. The horror that I saw there stayed with me for years.

"We came into the village from the lower end and found a hole in which the chief had been placed. He had been disemboweled and his throat cut from ear to ear. His wife and daughters had been brutalized and cut numerous times and then killed. This was something I thought we'd grown accustomed to, but the sight of that man and his family made me sick.

Dale Barnes

"This was the Cong's form of terror for submission. It always worked. From that point the things which I saw were not normal VC tactics. There was a ditch approximately 14 feet by 6 feet. In it was every villager. Each had been shot in the arms, legs, and finally either gut shot or head shot. Everyone was there, including babies and children. At the head of the ditch on the side was evidently the chieftain's daughter or someone of importance in the village. At the time of the raid by the VC she had been about to deliver a baby. They had split her from the vagina to her neck, taken the baby out and cut its throat. They laid it on her chest so she would have to watch it as it died. I was very angry at this. This was beyond war; this was torture of innocent people. This was not typical of the VC; this was something that was very sadistic.

"We tracked the group that did this horror for almost twenty-eight days and we finally caught them when they were rearming themselves with ammunition and medical supplies. In the middle of the group were two Russian advisors. I expected this type of activity more from the Chinese than the Viet Cong. I did not expect Russians to be there.

"They did not anticipate their capture. They were killed before we got back, but it wasn't by myself or my men. We had been tracked ourselves and by the time we got to the border, there was no way to get back without giving the Russians the Laotians.

"At many points we'd have double agents. As a matter of fact, some of our double agents were the best contacts because, to make themselves look good in our eyes, they would give us very important information on troop movement and other things, and they would expect the same from us. We would give them information but not true movements. It was an exchange of information, but we were getting the better end of the deal.

"I think the most traumatic experience I had was playing John Wayne. We were in camp for debriefing and were waiting for transfer to another camp to go on another mission. When we received some heavy firing, I grabbed the track, armored personnel carrier and headed out. I knew if I crushed the bamboo ramp, the rockets would not fire into the compound. The truck caught a knoll and tipped and a rocket slammed into the undercarriage and exploded, knocking me up to the top of a tree forty feet off the ground. My intestines were spilling over the ground, and I was surprised that I was not bleeding all over the place. In all, six men were killed, and I was the only one to survive intact. My driver lost both arms and a leg, and my gunner lost both arms and both legs.

"I still have shrapnel in me from that. When I go through a metal detector at the airport, I set it off. They wanted to give me a medical discharge, but

From Vietnam to Hell

Dale Barnes

I refused. I wanted to fight for my country, so after my time in the hospital I was sent back in.

"The VC used little children to some extent as distraction or booby traps. I did see some of our artillery fire sometimes fall short and kill children, but never on purpose. I would come into a village after some bombs and would see children and women dead and dying in the mud.

"When I returned to the States after my tour was up, I killed a hippie at the airport. I was walking down the area and saw a bunch of peace demonstrators. There were hippies carrying signs about the war in Vietnam which didn't bother me too much. This one man came at me as a blur, and I just reacted instinctively, the way I had been taught. I struck out and hit his neck and killed him instantly. There was a medic there, and we tried to save the boy's life, but it was useless. I did what I was trained to do. There were never any charges against me for this.

"As far as reacting to the people back here, my reactions were more on the line of hostile. I spent the next several months going across the Canadian and American border, staying away from everyone and everything.

Dale Barnes

I came back home, and my dad and I had a big argument. My dad was a military man, and he understood that I followed orders, but there was one part my dad did not understand. At the time, Nixon had just given a big speech about us not being in Laos. I was in the process of showing my dad my medals and papers that I'd gotten from Cambodia and Laos, and he did not believe I had been there. His commander-in-chief would not lie, he said. So, for a ten-year time, we didn't speak with each other.

"I got mad and burned everything. I wadded it all up and put kerosene to it and set it afire. Again, I told my dad what had gone on in the war, but he didn't want to listen.

"There was never any question but that we were right in going to Vietnam to fight. If you take a look at what was going on historically, if we had not intervened Thailand would not be free now. People in this country should look at the millions of people who have been slaughtered since we left. If that isn't reason enough for us to have been there, then I don't know what is.

"I don't feel the government of this country has done enough for the Vietnam vets. I still have a little hostility. I was with the first outreach program for the entire country. We had to fight for everything we got then, and we have to fight for what we get now.

"I went to Atlanta in 1983 at the request of the government. They kept me so drugged for eleven days that I didn't know who I was or where I was, and then they set me in the middle of a group of clerks, typists and others. I was the only combat soldier in the group. I left the hospital and hitch hiked home. I have been through two PTSD groups run by Jerry Washington here in Nashville which have helped me. They have gotten me in contact with myself and have given me an understanding of what I've gone through. I wouldn't go through a VA program because they just give drugs which I don't need. I'm tired of going to the damn hospital and when I get there, they give me these four thousand pills and say 'take these and you'll feel better.' I don't need that shit. I need honest understanding about what my problem is.

"I had taken drugs over in Vietnam and was drinking plenty of alcohol. It did not help because every time I sobered up, the problem was still there. I needed the alcohol to soothe my ego. I haven't had alcohol now in ten years and haven't had drugs in over five. It's taken a lot out of me, it really has. I've had time to heal a lot of problems since 'Nam. I'm still resentful of the government in the way they choose to deal with us. They allow us to die off and then those who are left are forgotten. At some point in time, they need to start treating these problems. We have ninety-eight thousand suicides out of a population of two-and-a-half million from Vietnam. That's an awful lot of people killing themselves.

From Vietnam to Hell

"PTSD is a real enemy that needs to be dealt with. Jerry Washington started putting together a group in 1982, called Base Camp, Inc., in Nashville, Tennessee. It's a center staffed by veterans. It offers no-nonsense counseling and referral services for all military veterans and their families. The service is free to all vets. It's a community-based, independent non-profit organization whose sole purpose is to help veterans.

"Base Camp provides a number of unique, veteran-centered programs that give vets a chance to get understanding healthful ways to work through their problems. They offer counseling, orientation, transitional housing and job placement and job maintenance counseling including assistance with permanent housing and independent living.

"War Stress (Post-Traumatic Stress Disorder) can take years to become evident and visible, especially when its symptoms have been repressed, when there has been no one to talk to about the war experiences.

The effects of War Stress vary among individuals. Some vets self-medicate with alcohol or other drugs, and some become over-achievers, trying to mask their symptoms through work. They try anything new: new jobs, new cities, new spouses. It often won't go away, and it can't be forgotten.

"I thank God that I came in contact with this group of people before it was too late. I used to have to knock myself against a brick wall to be able to sleep. Now I come for counseling twice a week, and it's much better. I'm getting ready to marry for the third time. This time will be the charm because this is the first time I've been able to live with some sort of normalcy. My first marriage was an attempt to be normal; it was a situation that we both ran into. She wanted to escape home, and I wanted to appear normal. My second marriage was one where I truly loved the lady, but she didn't care about me, and I was too dumb to see it. The lady I'm about to marry is wonderful. We have a better understanding of what's going on, and I feel I have a chance with this one.

"It's taken twenty-two years, but finally life is looking up for me. I've just written a book called *The Warrior Within*.

"It's a schizophrenic approach to the war. At the end of the soldier's training, a warrior is formed inside. So it's a dual personality born in everybody in the military whether they accept it or not. I sat down one day and realized that we all have a warrior inside us that got us through Vietnam. That's how we survived. When you take a normal personality and teach them to be mean, you create the warrior. Now that warrior can't go back to sleep so you have to deal with him day to day."

8

Jerry Barnet

U.S. Army

"I went into the service when I was in college. It was primarily a way of going from one place to the other in order to escape, for a change of pace. I went into the Army and became a military policeman. I had the opportunity to either stay there or go to Vietnam. I elected to go to Vietnam. At that time, I was nineteen and did not understand what a war really was. I had the concept of a free nation.

"I felt strongly and was quite caught up in the free world patriotism. I had a vision of what a male was supposed to do. I believed he should fight for his country and freedom. I pictured a little white house with a picket fence, kids, and cars in the garage. I was naïve, but back in the sixties, that was how I was brought up.

"I believed that if my country asked me to do something, I should do it, no questions asked. So, subsequently I enlisted and went to Vietnam. When I landed, I saw all these people around me going home. Not enthusiastically, or joyful, I would say they were more relieved than happy. I was taken to my unit and trained to outline the areas where supplies were being sent. We worked the harbor security and worked many jobs in the police field.

"I developed a very bad attitude while over there and found out I was prejudiced against authority, even though I didn't know it at the time. About three days after I got in the country, we had sniper fire. I've often wondered if it was real or just somebody playing around. The firing was directed toward our unit, and we didn't have any weapons. I was still in my khakis. I did not have a field uniform at all.

"I had a subtle feeling that there was no place safe because of the terrain and because of the way the war was being fought. One time I worked with a Vietnamese Nationalist policeman who I later found out was one of the Cong. In fact, he was the leader of the Viet Cong in that area. He was a national captain in the police force, and I wondered how to tell the good guys from the bad ones. They all looked the same; the only difference was the clothing they might have on at the time you saw them. You always had to be on guard, trusting no one.

"That really bothered me. I realized that the Vietnamese as a whole were less than human. As individuals, I had great respect for some of them. I saw many kids destroyed. That hurt me terribly. I remember looking with sorrow and hurt at these children, the orphans who ran around without any family to care for them. As we'd sit around the barracks, we wouldn't talk about the children; we'd talk about everything but that. The atrocities of war are hard. The memories never leave for long, and years later you still see those children. You still hear their cries. It was insanity, and you never talked about it to anyone, not even your closest buddy.

"I have great feelings of guilt. I suppressed any kind of feelings during the war and afterwards. Dealing with them was something I didn't understand. It was all subtle and would come out in my actions.

"I can recall a particular incident about which I became very enraged. It was a very unimportant happening. It was a verbal conflict between a Vietnamese lieutenant and some soldiers. It was just a stupid argument that left me bitter.

"I would go back to Vietnam if my country asked me to. I have no qualms about that. The devastation of the countryside and the people are still with me today. The country was very beautiful, with greenery and foliage everywhere. The cities were just like any other cities in the world. There was no big highrises like here in the United States, but still, they looked like any large city would. The heat was almost unbearable most of the time, but we got used to it. Once you were there, your body became used to the type weather they had. It was still uncomfortable, but it wasn't unbearable. It took me quite a while to adjust to it, but I finally did.

"I was ambushed a couple of times while over in Nam with the enemy. I was never involved in hand to hand combat, but was involved in several firing situations. I have no idea if I killed anyone or not. I have a suspicion that I did, but I never saw if my bullet or grenade actually killed someone.

"When I came back to the United States, I felt slighted. I felt used by my government. I felt a tremendous amount of anger and frustration. I did not look at it like that at the time. I was unable to express that feeling back then. There was a loneliness and shock associated with coming back from the hot temperature over there to the cold climate back here.

"I took a plane from San Diego to Nashville, and there was an anti-war group demonstrating there. One of them was quite uncomplimentary in her comments to me. I took it personally that she would call me a baby killer.

Jerry Barnet

Jerry Barnet

I became so angry. I was in a seething rage inside and wanted to lash out at everyone. I chose to ignore it, but it was hard to walk by them. It may not have been the best thing in the world for me, but it's the way I wanted to handle it.

"When I reached home, I sat up and talked to my mother six or seven hours. I don't know if she understood my feelings or not and I never talked about it again to her. I medicated myself tremendously, and began to drink a lot. It seemed to ease the pain. The drinking was a symptom of the underlying problems that I had to face. My natural reaction was to medicate myself and live the façade that I did all those years. I lived normally on the outside, but underneath I knew something was wrong; something was bothering me that I didn't understand.

"My wife had left, my kids were gone, I didn't have the normal support system and I was no longer able to suppress my feelings. In my particular case, I started dealing with the issues of alcoholism. I stopped drinking and, while I no longer had the alcohol, I still had the problems.

"I believe the American government has done the best it could under the circumstances. The government could provide more useful services, however. Knowing how to use the system to obtain those services is something that I'm interested in learning for myself. I believe they are there; it's just knowing how to get them. That is a challenge in itself.

"Three years ago I started coming to Basecamp here in Nashville. It has helped me a lot. I honestly believe that had I not come here, I would be dead. I read an article in the paper about Basecamp, and I gave them a call and offered my services. I was in a stage of denial. I felt that I didn't have any problems left at that time.

"At Basecamp, we talk to others who have gone through what we did and it helps a great deal. We find alternative ways of looking at things, and I look at the other points of view. My life is getting back on track now, thanks to Basecamp. I do not regret my military service in Vietnam. There are some things I wish hadn't happened, but they did. It may not be fair, but in reality they did happen.

"Last year I went to the Wall in Washington, D.C. It was a painful, yet very healthy and wholesome experience. The pain, the feelings and remorse have now become much more acceptable than before. I had a very open hostility to the wall. I didn't think it was an appropriate monument. My views have now changed. I could not think of anything that could be any better. I think it's a beautiful piece of art that relays the feelings of the veterans.

"I looked up names of people I had known were alive when I left and their names weren't on the Wall. One day I will go back to see the Wall again."

Gary Cone

U.S. Army

"I went to school just outside Fort Campbell, Kentucky. My father was in the Army and was stationed there for six years. I had an older brother who died at the age of fifteen and two sisters. We traveled from base to base, and I was moved from one school to another, always having to make different friends and begin anew. I did not like moving, but that was the way we lived.

"During my school years, I was far above my classmates. I was rarely absent from school because I liked it. My I.Q. was well above average, and I was referred to as a genius by those who were aware of my scholastic efforts.

"I remember my father as a harsh and unlikeable man. When my father was stationed overseas, my mother would take us children to Lake Village in southeast Arkansas. She would often make our clothes. While we had plenty to eat, there was never much left over for the extra things.

"In nineteen sixty-six I was graduated from high school and later joined the Army. After basic training I was sent to Germany. I then requested to be sent to Vietnam.

"I had to wonder if I would act like a coward when I saw my first battle. I think we were all thinking these thoughts as we flew to Nam.

"I was nineteen years old when I first got to Vietnam. I had just come from Germany where I had been for fifteen months. I didn't really know what I was getting into, and I didn't care. I just wanted to get out of Germany, so I volunteered to go. When I got there, I found that the atmosphere was much less restrictive. It didn't matter how you got something done as long as you did it. I was a supply specialist with the first infantry division. I did not see much actual combat, but I saw the mortars they shot as we ducked for cover.

"We didn't have the same spirit of closeness that they had in the other wars. We spent twelve months in Vietnam. Everyone left at different times, so someone who only had a month before being shipped home would not want to go out in the fields to fight. Those who were new there and had three hundred days left would be sent out.

"I first started taking drugs when they were given to me by the Army medics. A big bag of opium could be bought for ten dollars. We would take a gas mask bag and fill it up with drugs. On guard duty the medics would give us a handful of amphetamines to keep us awake.

"Vietnam was not a pretty place. The Emergency Room tent looked like a slaughter house. You could not keep the blood mopped up. There were many boys with severed arms and legs. Many were gut shot and screaming to their mothers or girlfriends. I'd see men with stumps where their arms should have been, and I felt horror. Some had brains seeping down their faces and stark terror in their eyes. I knew they were conscious of how bad they were wounded. It was like watching a horror movie.

"The rats were as big as small dogs, and we had to sleep with our heads under covers. If we didn't, we would be bitten. We could not get rid of the rats. The more we killed, the more they seemed to multiply.

"When I first got off the plane, the heat took my breath away. The smell was overpowering. We could smell urine, sweat and mold. Everything was wet because it rained most of the time. You had to walk through the mud, sleep in the mud and even eat in the mud. You were lucky if your combat boots stayed dry. Most of the time you could feel the mud sloshing around your feet.

"I'd dream of a hot shower, sheets on my bed, and a decent meal in a dry place. These pictures soon faded as we struggled just to stay alive.

"The horrors of war were too much for me to cope with. Women and young children were frequently befriended and subsequently caught hiding grenades in their clothing. It seemed as if we couldn't trust anyone and had to be constantly alert. The children seemed innocent, but the Vietcong would use them to hide bombs. They had no regard for human life, not even for their own children. The heat was always over one hundred degrees, and the bugs bit day and night. No comforts of home existed, but we learned to live with it. We had to sleep on the ground, sometimes with water up to our necks. Ants would crawl on our bodies and many of the men got malaria and dysentery. It was to be a long time before I would sleep in a bed with sheets and blankets.

"I rose to the rank of staff sergeant and earned a commendation. Taking body bags from the fields, some of which contained the bodies of my friends, was one of the many things in my line of duty. My sleep was disrupted by visions of a buddy's head being blown off or dying women and children I had seen left in the fields. The Viet Cong would often torture and cut the children in half. Women often suffered the same fate. I started taking speed and opium. They were inexpensive, and it made life easier to cope with. At times, such as when I pulled fifty-three straight nights of guard duty on the base perimeter and had to stay awake, the drugs felt like a necessity to me. I would smoke marijuana and other drugs all the time. It seemed like everybody over there did drugs to stay sane.

"After a year in Vietnam, I was honorably discharged and went home to go to college. I was twenty years old and had to use fake identification to buy beer. I was old enough to fight and kill for my country, but not old enough to buy a beer once I came home. It was pitiful, but that's the way it was. Once home, people treated me badly, so I stayed away from them. I wouldn't listen to the war on the television or radio; I didn't care about it anymore. It was over as far as I was concerned.

"Over the years I've come to think the war was stupid. You don't go into a place and fight for an idea and then not try to win the war. You are sacrificing fifty thousand troops in the meantime. Now the main thing I see is people in the National Guard. I think more highly of those who went to Canada to avoid the war, than I do somebody who joined the National Guard to avoid the war.

"I majored in banking and finance and graduated in nineteen seventy-two. I did well enough on my law test to seriously consider going to law school, but I continued taking drugs of various types. I found that I could not stop. It was a way of life to me. I couldn't find a job anywhere. It seemed like no one needed me. I decided to buy a pistol and start robbing stores to survive. I successfully robbed a checkout stand at the grocery store, then continued the habit.

"I decided to attend law school at the University of Tulsa, with my GI bill paying the cost. I met and fell in love with Glenda Cale, a student at the University of Arkansas. We soon became engaged.

"Vietnam still stuck with me, and I found it difficult to talk about my problems with my friends. Glenda thought that I was dealing in drugs, as I always seemed to have money. I was, however, getting money to support my drug habit from robberies of gas stations and convenience stores. Two months before I was to start school, I was arrested and sentenced to twenty-five years in an Oklahoma prison for armed robbery. Glenda and I broke the engagement since I would be in prison.

"I hadn't been in prison long when my father died. Soon afterwards, I learned that my girlfriend was raped and killed by an escapee from a Nebraska mental hospital. The world had stopped for me, and I took more drugs to erase the pain. Friends turned me on to heroin again. I began to mainline. I couldn't find any reason to straighten out my life.

From Vietnam to Hell

"Prison had changed me. I was bitter about my life and about the lost years I had spent incarcerated. I was always high and never wanted to come down. Whenever I closed my eyes, I would see the Viet Cong. I would see the bodies of children and women lying tortured and maimed in the fields. I never knew what was going on around me and barely knew what I was doing.

"Once paroled I tried to put my life in order. I was accepted in the Arkansas Law School. I wanted a career in law. Even though I was a convicted felon and could not be admitted to the bar, I still wanted to pursue a career in the field.

"I had a few months before school would begin, and I tried unsuccessfully to find work. There were no jobs that I could find with my record. I then turned to the trade that I knew: robbery. I chose drug stores as I needed drugs as well as cash. I never wanted to hurt anyone. I believed all of this would stop once I started school. I spent a few weeks in Hawaii, strung out on cocaine and losing touch with reality. Before the fall term began, I started my return to Arkansas.

"On August 8, 1980, I robbed a grocery store. The next day I went into another store and filled a bag with over $100,000 worth of jewelry. I was seen leaving the parking lot and was chased by the police. I finally abandoned my car and ran on foot, with the police fast behind me. Gunfire was exchanged, and an officer was wounded. I eluded the police and spent the night in a burned out building. Police closed in and fired tear gas into the structure, but I hid in the fireplace and they gave up. The long night of fear from the police, the shooting, and the tear gas brought my mind swiftly back to the jungles of Vietnam. It was over one hundred degrees that day, and the sweat poured down into my eyes. I had not eaten in several days, and I actually believed I was back in the war.

"I broke into a house, entering from the back door. When I left the house that day, two people inside were dead. I don't remember killing them, but I know I must have. All I can remember is the police chasing me. I remember thinking I was in the jungle of Vietnam, with the Cong chasing me, trying to kill me before I could kill them. I left the house and went to my sister's home. It was not long before I was arrested.

I stood trial and was given the death sentence. I don't think I was represented very well with my court-appointed attorney. He did not adequately describe my drug problem or PTSD. Since I robbed drug stores and always carried drugs, they assumed I was a drug seller instead of a drug user. I hadn't bought drugs from anyone who could get on the stand and say I used them. They just assumed I was selling the drugs I stole. If I could have proven my drug addiction in court, I probably wouldn't have gotten the death sentence. The attorney just didn't bring up these important issues. I would still be in prison, but I don't think I'd be on death row.

"I think the fact that Vietnam was the high point of my life is sad. I didn't come home in a body bag, I didn't come home in a wheel chair, I'm not missing limbs, and even though I thought I had come home a complete person, it's evident that I didn't. I don't think I deserve to die for my crime because I know the state of mind that I was in at the time of the murders. They certainly weren't lucid or sane in any manner.

"Today I sit on Tennessee's death row. Because no one believed that post-traumatic stress disorder was real, the men who returned from the war didn't receive help to get over the horrors they had seen. Maybe if help had come earlier, two people wouldn't have died that day and I would not be sitting on death row. Is it my fault that I became hooked on drugs in the jungles of Vietnam and later thought in my mind I was back there? I don't know the answer; I just feel the government didn't do enough for us who fought for our country."

Nelson

U.S. Marine Corps

"I was married and had three children when I received orders to Vietnam. We were stationed in Cherry Point, North Carolina, and I couldn't bring myself to tell my wife that I had to leave. A song was out at that time called, "Hello Vietnam," so I bought a copy of it and played it over and over. Shirley didn't realize I was trying to tell her that I was going to leave. I finally had to tell her and the kids that I, along with our closest friends, had all received orders for Vietnam.

"Shirley was from Concord, New Hampshire, so I took them all back there where she would have family members to lean on while I was overseas. I remember looking at my wife, wishing I could stop the tears that streamed down her cheeks as I got on the plane. The war was going to take me many miles away from her and the kids. It was the first time since we had been married that we had been apart. I knew I would worry constantly about her and the kids. She wasn't used to being alone and, even with family nearby, I still had a bad feeling in my stomach.

"I was a sergeant and a squad leader. It was my duty to take my men out on night patrol, killing the Cong in the jungles. We never knew who the enemy was. Here, the people all looked the same, and the only difference was in the clothes they wore.

"One night I took thirteen men out on patrol and the Viet Cong ambushed us from behind. We never knew what hit us. I watched as my men were slaughtered; only four of us returned to the base. I told the commander I didn't want to take any more men out; I didn't want to be responsible for their deaths.

"I became what was known as a mole. I would sleep during the day and at night would take just a knife to kill the Cong. It was horrible. I remember crying. I was scared, and I wondered why we were there. I had to kill young men and women. I was tired of the killing. No one told me it would be like this.

Nelson

"Every night I would say to myself that I didn't want to die. I'd take out my wife's picture and talk to her. I'd tell her I was going to come home to her in one piece. No matter what I had to do, I was going to come home. I would see her face, and the kids as they would hug me at night, and I'd feel such loneliness. Then the fire would come in, and we would jump up and kill over and over again. We did what we had to do. It was a fight. I was a Marine, and we thought we'd save the world and make the people as free as we were back in the States.

"It didn't take long to learn that you couldn't trust anyone in the jungles. The civilians were sometimes caught in the middle and would be killed by one side or the other. Even the children and women would hide grenades. Still, we found some Vietnamese people who were friendly. Many men fell in love with the delicate beauty of the Vietnamese women.

"Fighting in Vietnam is something that no one will ever forget. I know I never will. There are fear and confusing thoughts because you fight face to face. Americans are taught not to kill, but there we were told to kill them all. Sometimes the enemy was invisible, and you couldn't see who you were fighting. Then, other times you could see the hate-filled faces just inches from your own. It was kill or be killed. We had our own air support, but with the dense jungle it was hard for them to help at times.

"I remember one time while on patrol we came upon a little girl with a bamboo pole stuck up her rectum. She was screaming and in a great deal of pain. It was plain to see that she couldn't survive. The other men stood staring at her, not knowing what to do. I picked up my rifle and put her out of her misery. I'll never forget that little girl's face, and I can still hear her screams of pain. My own daughter was just her age, and I would think, what if the fighting was over there? What if it were my daughter hanging like that, screaming in pain and begging someone to help?

"I would drink to forget; then we'd go back in the jungle and kill again and again. At least while I was half drunk, it didn't seem so bad. I remember when I first got there, we were told to kill all who wore black pajamas. Then they told us they had to be armed. Then we were told they had to shoot first. Eventually we didn't know when we could shoot. Sometimes the guys would wait too long, and they were killed. You had to shoot first, or you'd never make it.

"The Cong would set up flares and come at us. We could see the whites of their eyes and the crazy smiles on their faces as they screamed, 'Malines, you die.' They couldn't speak English, so the word Marine came out as Maline. We were scared all the time. Some of the guys would never admit that they cried, or that they were scared. It's not a John Wayne movie; it's real life. It's horror.

19

From Vietnam to Hell

"The worst thing that happened was one night when I was standing between two close friends. We heard the Viet Cong coming and tried to jump in the fox holes. I heard an explosion and saw pieces of bodies flying in the air. You could hear them screaming as they came. We shot blindly, not seeing in the blackness of the night. The noise was deafening and the sky lit up like a fourth of July fireworks display. Then, as suddenly as it began, it stopped. When I looked over, one of my friends was gone. There wasn't anything left of him. He had been blown to bits. I was crying and covered with mud and blood. My friend was dead, gone forever in a moment of violence.

"I began drinking to blot out the horror that surrounded me. Other men took drugs to forget what was happening all around us. Cocaine and marijuana were plentiful and cheap. The guys stayed high so they wouldn't have to feel the pain of the dead and dying. They stayed high to blot out the horror of seeing their best friends blown into little pieces. I did everything I could to survive. I would write to my wife every night and tell her how much I loved her. I didn't tell her about the things I saw and the things I did. We were in another world, and no one could understand what we were going through unless they were with us.

"One of the hardest things was knowing that little children were being used to kill our men. The Cong would give a small child a grenade and tell it to go into a bunch of GIs and then blow it up. Women would also do this and, of course, they would die in the process. We eventually began to kill the women and children if they came near us. You couldn't tell if they were friendly.

"I remember one day we were walking by a bunch of women and children. They were laughing and talking and the children would run up to the GIs and beg for chocolate. They loved the chocolate bars the Marines would pass out and would beg for some every chance they got. Once the men were almost past, a very pregnant woman walked up to the middle of the line and blew herself up along with half the platoon. It was crazy. We were here to save these people from Communism and they hated us. They would side with the Viet Cong and kill those who came to free them. I still can't believe they did this. If I hadn't seen these things with my own eyes, I never would have believed them.

"One by one, my friends were killed. I couldn't believe that I'd never see them again. One minute we'd be there talking and having a drink; the next minute they were blown to bits. I would walk by men with no arms or legs, lying in a pool of blood. Sometimes these men would still be alive and I'd retch.

"I reached one man as he lay there with no limbs. He was still alive and

20

seemed to know there was nothing left of his body. He begged me not to let his family know how he died. Then he closed his eyes and was gone. I felt relief that he was out of his misery, and that it wasn't me lying there. I felt guilt because I was glad it was him and not me, but I guess we all felt the same way.

"The Vietnamese rode motorbikes and pedal rickshaws all over the towns. They would always travel with their belongings and livestock. I felt sorry for the children but was afraid to get close to them. I had seen grenades strapped to the little ones before. The Viet Cong felt the children were expendable. I could not believe people were willing to kill their own children in this war. The dirty streets with open markets stank. They stunk to high heaven. It was like a carnival atmosphere, with the Vietnamese trying to make money from the Americans. There were massage parlors, whorehouses and black market items. Every other shop was a bar. The men would bring a girl up to a GI and try to sell her. Some of the girls were very dirty.

"Then the day came when my commander called me into his office. My wife had taken an overdose of sleeping pills, and they were sending me home. I was on the next flight out to the States and home. I remember the pain I felt as I saw my wife again, knowing she had tried to commit suicide because she couldn't bear the thought of me being in Vietnam.

"I decided to leave the Marine Corps to be with my family. I had spent seven years in the Marines and was planning to make it a career. I loved my wife more than the Corps and decided to take care of her. We moved to North Carolina, and I found work as a mechanic. My son Trevor was born that year. We then had two girls and two boys. We bought a new home near Asheville, North Carolina, and were very happy.

"I thought I'd be a hero when I came home. I know a lot of kids went to Canada in order to avoid Vietnam. I called them cowards. I, like thousands of others, had to go and fight for my country. I thought that it was the American thing to do. Now this same country that I had fought for was telling me I was a nothing. I was a baby killer and should never have been there. I wonder what they'd have called us if we hadn't obeyed orders, if we'd all gone to Canada.

"I couldn't believe what some people were yelling at me. I remember people telling me about coming home from the Korean War. The parades up and down the city streets, big bands playing and people from all over the world approaching men in uniforms. These soldiers were heroes, and they were welcomed home with open arms. They'd get free coffee in restaurants, perhaps even a free meal. When I came home, however, I had a different homecoming. No one cheered, no bands played and there weren't any parades marching by cheering us on. No one wanted to talk about Vietnam or the men and boys who were over there dying.

"Then, I began drinking all the time. I never missed work because of the drinking, but as soon as work was over, I would drink. I didn't want to go anywhere or do anything with my wife or the kids. For eight years this went on, and I could tell Shirley was getting tired of the constant drinking and crying. As soon as I'd had a couple of drinks, I would see those faces and I felt hate. I would see the little girl I had shot, and I asked God to forgive me. Tears would fall, and I'd find myself crying.

"I felt my life was drifting away, and I had no control. At night I would dream of the things I had done in Vietnam and the things I had seen. I'd look down at my hands and see blood. I couldn't erase those faces, and I couldn't erase the blood. I couldn't talk to my wife about these things because I was ashamed of the way I had been. I knew I was hurting the kids, but I couldn't help myself. The more I dreamed, the more I drank. The more I drank, the more I cried. I know Shirley tried to understand. She'd ask me to talk to her, but I was afraid she would hate me.

"The end finally came when my oldest son found himself in trouble with the law. He was with a friend who committed a robbery and killed the shopkeeper. I advised my son Jeff to turn himself in because I still believed in the United States justice system.

"I was drinking and went to the sheriff's department. My son shouldn't have turned himself in because he could not prove he hadn't gone inside with the other boy. Although they knew he hadn't committed the murder, he was given the death sentence along with the other boy. This was the end of my marriage. Shirley couldn't handle the fact that I had advised Jeff to come in and take his punishment. He had never been in trouble before and was a good kid. She divorced me even though I begged her not to. I said I'd never drink again if only she'd give me another chance. I knew I had said this many times in the past, and at the time I said it, I believed I could stop.

"My son was taken to death row in Nashville, Tennessee, and Shirley moved to be with him. My two daughters stayed in North Carolina with the rest of the family. My oldest daughter, Tina, married and became pregnant with her first child. Her life was going pretty well. Laurie, my youngest daughter, was in the middle of a divorce and had a baby girl named Jessica.

"I went back to New York and lived with my mother. I continued drinking. I didn't even try to work. I just begged the family for money. I was constantly in a drunken state, until even my family didn't want me around. I didn't bathe or brush my teeth. I knew I stank, and no one wanted to be near me. I'd see them roll their eyes every time I would come near. In the beginning they tried to help me, but I didn't want their help. I just wanted to drink. I would call Shirley, and she'd talk to me on the phone. She'd try to convince me to go to AA, but I wouldn't listen. She really cared about me, and I knew she tried to understand what I was going through.

"I loved her and wanted to get my family back, but not enough to stop drinking. She told me she still loved me, but it wasn't the same love she had felt for me when we first married. My kids wouldn't talk to me when I was drunk.

"The day came when I finally went to AA. I got a job and cleaned up. During the summer I would go to Tennessee to visit with Shirley and Jeff's daughter, Maria. Shirley had adopted Maria when Jeff was put on death row. She always let me come and stay with them whenever I wasn't drinking. It hurt. It hurt to see Shirley and know she wasn't mine anymore. I loved her more than anything in the world. We had been married for seventeen years and divorced for ten, but I still felt the same love every time I looked at her.

"I don't know why I started drinking again, but I did. It just happened one day. I had been exposed to Agent Orange and got a small settlement, but the government didn't really want to acknowledge that they had caused it. They thought the small payoff was all they needed to do.

"My son Trevor came up to New York to help me stop drinking, and I tried over and over. But I just felt the need to drink again. My oldest son is on the last appeal, and we're hoping and praying for a miracle to save him. He has never hurt anyone, and he sits on death row. I have guilt feelings about that also. I should have told him to run, but I didn't know the system was for the rich only. I didn't know they wanted $100,000 to handle a murder case. Life has no meaning anymore; it's just something to get through.

"Now I'm drinking again. I don't feel like a man anymore. Vietnam took that away from me. I feel like dying, but I'm too cowardly to take my own life. I realize I suffer from post-traumatic stress disorder, but people don't understand. They don't believe it's a real disease that kills. They ask why the servicemen in the other wars didn't have it. I have no answers. It may be related to the fact that the men from other wars were brought back to the United States on boats. It would take months for them to finally arrive in California and by that time they had talked to their buddies about the horrors they had seen. They had talked it all out. With us, it was different. One day we were killing the Cong; the next day, we were back in the States.

"No one wanted to listen to us. No one would let us get it out of our systems. We had to kill children in this war, and that's something most men can't forget. I know I can't. I just drink to forget. I'm waiting until the day I die when all pain and memory will be gone."

Robert Davis

U.S. Army

"When I first went to Vietnam I was scared that I would not come back alive. I was in Echo Company, the same division as Lieutenant Kelly of the My Lai Massacre. My first impression of Vietnam was it looked like prehistoric times when dinosaurs lived. The jungle with all the greenery and the sandy beaches was beautiful.

"When I first landed there, we had to have special training. The Army would train us to avoid land mines. They would train us for seven days before we could go in actual combat.

"They sent me to a place called L Z West which was thirty miles from DaNang and sixty miles from Chu Lai. I went in as an indirect fire and mortar man. They were in need of mortarmen so I got lucky. I could stay on the fire support base instead of going out in the field for hand-to-hand combat. When the troops would go out and look for the Cong, however, they would come back to the fire base and regroup. The enemy got so mad because we were hitting them and running that they waited until the time was right and thousands of them tried to overrun the fire support base. We had only two hundred men on top of the hill but we fought them from that night until the next morning. A prisoner told us that they had over six thousand men.

"Every third bunker had sixty machine guns and two cases of grenades on it. They took me out of mortars and put me on a bunker to direct fire. I spotted the enemy when they came up the hill. I saw a head pop up and then a body would crawl on top of another body and come through the wire. They would lie on the razor-sharp wire knowing they could cut themselves, but they didn't seem to care; they just kept coming.

"I looked to the hill and the enemy was marching in columns which indicated that they were sure they would defeat us. But we had a surprise for them. The four-point deuce was firing elimination rounds, the eighty-one mortars were dropping high explosive rounds, and inside our perimeter, as close to me as twenty feet, mortars were dropping.

Robert Davis

"We fired a 106 rifle, a beehive round which is against the Geneva Convention. We fired it because we thought we were going to be overrun. It was a giant shotgun, and the shell was fired out of a cannon. It had small steel darts.

"I had to keep down to keep the shrapnel from hitting me. I saw the Cong get caught in the barbwire and hang there, not able to free themselves. I could hear their screams. They were saying they surrendered. We were not allowed to take prisoners. There were many Cong, and we were told to shoot them.

"One of the worst things about the jungles was the sight of the inch-long black ants crawling over the dead bodies. When the men were dead or dying, the ants would eat the blood.

"After one attack there were thousands of bodies lying all over the hill. There were so many we didn't know what to do with them. The Army called in the Corps engineers in the morning and brought in bulldozers. They dug a big hole with the machines and we put the dead bodies in it. The bulldozers put dirt over them while we watched. It was gruesome, but it had to be done. I can still see those bodies lying one on top of another. The smell of death haunts me to this day. We would still find body parts months later while walking on guard duty. I remember one day I found a human skull with hair still on it, and I felt sick.

"The North Vietnamese Army was like we were. They would fight to the end. They wouldn't hit and run like the Viet Cong. The Cong would hit us and run before we could get back, then hit again, and run. The NVA stood and fought until one or the other was dead. They wouldn't surrender.

"I was so scared and didn't think I'd ever make it back to the States, but finally I did. When I came back, my war was over, or so I thought. I was hooked on marijuana because I had smoked so much in Vietnam. It had kept me from losing my mind. I had never seen a dead person before, and I'd never killed anyone either. I had to kill over there, so I had to be high all the time in order to survive. Killing is not the easiest thing to do.

"I hadn't known about drugs before I went over there. The Vietnamese would give us the drugs, telling us they would make us feel good. The Vietnamese would give us marijuana, heroin, alcohol, or anything else we wanted. When we came back to the States, it wasn't legal, and many of the men would spend time in prisons for doing drugs. The cost of drugs in the States was high and many turned to crime to pay for their habit. I think giving us drugs was the communist way of weakening us so we couldn't win the war. When I would see the communists supplying us with drugs over

25

From Vietnam to Hell

Robert Davis

there, I was shocked. I believe that the drugs today are brought in by the communists to weaken the United States.

"When I first came back, people would call me murderer, rapist, son of a bitch and a lot worse. They had the wrong opinion of GIs who came back from Vietnam. We were treated like dirt. No one could understand the GIs because we were different. The Vietnam War was altogether different from the other wars. They knew who they were fighting, and we didn't. In Vietnam they used children and women to fight; they would use anything they could.

"When I first came back I would have flashbacks. I became uncomfortable when people would walk close behind me. I couldn't handle frustrations and felt anger all the time. I worked at a cigar factory for seven years without any trouble. No one knew I had been in Vietnam because I didn't want anyone to know. Then the factory closed down, and I moved to Wisconsin.

"Things didn't go very well there, and people began talking to me about Vietnam. They would ask what I had done, and then I'd usually end up in a fight. I finally had a nervous breakdown and was put in the VA hospital. I spent three months in therapy.

Robert Davis

"My wife and children tried to survive on welfare. Once I was discharged from the hospital, Social Security took over and got my family back on its feet. In nineteen eighty I started to get disability insurance from the government. It was one hundred percent service connected.

"I blame the Army for what it has done to me. I remember hitting a sergeant one time after he hit me first. I lost a stripe over it. He could hit me, but I wasn't supposed to hit him back.

"I think the government has helped a few vets, but there are eighty thousand that don't have any place to live still on the streets. They don't have jobs or people who care about them. People just call us drug addicts, and no one wants to help us. I think they should get these vets off the streets, find jobs for them and help them to get their lives back together again. Thirty thousand Vietnam vets have committed suicide because they're not accepted in today's world.

"My wife left me soon after I came home. I blame it on the war and the way I became. I always wanted to talk about the war and would wake her up at night to talk about the fight on the hill and the things I'd seen. She took it for fifteen years, but then she couldn't take it any more. A Vietnam vet is hard to live with.

"I still have flashbacks, and I still have dreams. The dreams are very real. One night I had a dream that I was running out of ammunition, and I was running to get more. I woke up at the bottom of the stairs. I had broken my leg. That's how real my dreams are.

"I still have a good relationship with my ex-wife. She lets me see my kids on the weekends. I call her often to talk. She's remarried, now, but I've come to accept it. I live in Murfreesboro, Tennessee, in a brick house with my friend Norman who is also a Vietnam vet. We've been friends now for nine years, and it's great. We sit and talk and drink coffee. It helps a lot to have someone to talk to about what we went through. If I didn't have him to talk to, I'd be sitting here alone, just staring at the walls or talking to myself.

"I donated forty pen and ink drawings to help a woman who needs open heart surgery which is expected to cost seventy-five thousand dollars. I felt like I was doing something to help others. It's my way of paying back for what I did in Vietnam, and it's great therapy. It's bringing me back to life.

"I have my art work scattered over Kentucky, Indiana, Illinois, Wisconsin, and now in Tennessee. I'm sending Senator Jim Sassor ten prints, because he called the newspaper to have them do a story on me and my art work. I have given hundreds of prints away to people all over the world.

"I could never talk about Vietnam before because I was too scared to talk about the things I'd done over there. But now with the help of my psychiatrist and the medication they have me on, I can function. I've been completely disabled since nineteen seventy-nine and don't trust myself to drive a car, but in every way I have begun to live again. I have a new life ahead of me. I started writing to a woman who is forty-two years old, and we have become great friends. I proposed to her, and she accepted. Although I've never met her in person, I feel I can trust her. She's faced hard times and been kicked around. This wonderful woman is named Joyce and is originally from Virginia. She's going to spend her life with me. My ex-wife has talked to her, and they get along fine. I'm happy that I'm now going to have a new life, a new beginning."

Fred

U.S. Navy

Fred was born in Washington County, Virginia, on March 20, 1945. His father was in the Army at the time and was stationed in Europe. For most of Fred's younger years, his father was not around, but he wanted to be in the service when he grew up.

"My brother and I were living with my father in Wilmington, North Carolina, when I turned seventeen in nineteen sixty-two. I wanted to join the Navy, but my father wouldn't agree. One day while he was away, I packed a few belongings and hitched back to my mother's home in Bristol, Virginia. She signed for me to join the Navy, where I was to remain until nineteen seventy-four.

"While in the Navy, I served with the Navy's SEAL team in Vietnam. The death and destruction I witnessed there haunts me to this day. I was married and had a baby daughter when I received orders to Vietnam. I was stationed on a ship in Norfolk, Virginia, and seldom went to sea because of the ship's particular type and job. I had learned that the Navy was looking for volunteers from my rating specialty to train as SEAL team members for duty in Vietnam, so I volunteered and was accepted. I didn't tell my wife that I had volunteered to go so that my brother David, who had received orders to go, wouldn't have to. They very seldom sent two from one family to Vietnam at the same time and I didn't want my brother to be there.

"I was sent to Fort Bragg, North Carolina, where I was trained in low-level parachute jumps, then to New London, Connecticut for training on how to exit a submarine while submerged. From New London I went to California for SEAL school. Here I was trained and became expert in jungle warfare and survival, diving, weapons, hand to hand combat, and killing. It was here I became skilled in killing with a knife, crossbow, guns, and my hands; all, I was told, would be put to use in Vietnam. After I had trained for twenty-six weeks, I, along with eleven other graduates, was designated as SEAL TEAM 5 and sent to Vietnam. We flew to Saigon aboard a military flight and arrived just after dark. Accompanying our group were three civilians who were "advisors." We suspected they were from the CIA, but they never admitted it. They would be with us for our one-year tour.

"After a quick meal, we were flown by helicopter to the small village of Can Tho in the Mekong Delta, which would be our base of operations. Immediately upon arriving we were briefed by more "CIA-types" on an up-coming mission and began more training in low-level parachute jumps, this time with a different type of parachute, and from helicopters. After a few days we were briefed again and boarded our helicopters and headed west, destination unknown. During the flight we checked and doublechecked weapons and supplies and practiced our hand signals, as once on the ground, talking would be strictly forbidden.

"After what seemed like hours, we jumped into the jungle, regrouped, and headed for a point several miles away. Arriving at our destination, we were met by a dozen or so Army Special Forces men and were again briefed on why we were there and what our job would be. It was then we learned we were in Cambodia, and illegally. Our mission was to enter a village some miles away and eliminate certain individuals who were known Viet Cong and to destroy the village and get back into South Vietnam unnoticed. The "CIA-type" with us gathered all personal items that could identify us as Americans, gave each of us a cyanide capsule to be used in case of capture, briefed us once again, and we were off.

"We arrived at our destination two nights later and entered the sleeping village from three directions. There were four guards around the village that fell prey to our expertly taught killing techniques. My first taste of enemy blood came as I slit the throat of a youngster about seventeen years old. Finding the VC we had come for, they were dispatched in a like manner, and we set fire to the village. Women and children began to scream and run from their grass huts. We were "advised" by the "CIA-type" to kill all the people or we could be discovered. Reluctantly and with great speed, we shot and killed over thirty innocent people. I felt sick as I heard the screams of the dying, the children, the women. I had never dreamed we'd have to kill women and children and their faces haunt me today.

"These types of missions went on month after month. Our questions about killing women and children were answered with, 'it's necessary.' I didn't come to Vietnam to kill women and children, but I did what I was told was my duty. After each mission I would vomit for hours and beg God to forgive us for what we were doing.

"After a while, the killing didn't seem to bother me anymore except when I slept. I could see the faces of those who died by my hand before me:

innocent faces begging to live, so many faces. What kind of war was this that we had to kill unarmed women and children?

"Night after night I lay awake, never able to get a good night's sleep. The unbearable heat was oppressing, and every kind of creature you could imagine slithered around the jungles. It seemed like it was raining the whole time we were there.

"I survived that year in Vietnam and returned to my wife and daughter a different person than I had been when I left. My nightmares continued, and I'd have spells of crying and a fear that I might lose control one day. I thought I might never stop crying over those faces that kept haunting my dreams, and my waking time. I felt like I was nobody, that God would never forgive the horrible things I had been forced to do in 'Nam.

"I was afraid to tell my wife that I had killed children the age of my own child. I feared she would hate me and never want me near her or my daughter again if she knew. It was torture to keep it all in, but I couldn't take the chance of losing her love and maybe having her leave me because of it. Our marriage eventually broke up anyway. She couldn't stand the constant crying and mood swings. I didn't know at the time that I had post-traumatic stress disorder. I just felt I was in hell with nowhere to turn for comfort.

"I left the Navy in nineteen seventy-four and went from job to job. I was never satisfied with being in one place very long. I had nightmares; sweat would pour down my face and I was chilled. I felt angry most of the time and didn't know why or what I was mad at.

"I had a sense of helplessness and didn't know where to turn for help. I didn't believe that anyone could understand my feelings, and I couldn't talk about my time in Vietnam. Almost anything could make me remember the jungle of Vietnam: the sound of a helicopter, rainy days and nights, or the smell of urine. I didn't know what was wrong, but was told I suffered from post-traumatic stress disorder. This is not a mental illness, but a reaction to the extreme stress we were placed under during and after the Vietnam War.

"Sometimes I felt like killing myself, but I always stopped before I could do it. I didn't like having these feelings, but they came when I least expected them. I remember feeling guilty that I had come home while so many of my friends were killed in the jungle.

"I decided to move back to the old hometown and settle down there close to my mother and sisters. I married twice more, only to have these marriages fail also. I joined the Army National Guard but left after four years because they again were training me to kill. I'd had enough killing to last me a lifetime and didn't want any part in it anymore.

"My Navy and Army Guard time totaled sixteen years fighting for my country; sixteen years that will haunt me until God removes me from this

From Vietnam to Hell

wicked world. Twenty-one years have passed since Vietnam, but the memories and nightmares continue. Those ever-present faces remain burned into my brain.

"I've told my closest friends about my time in Vietnam, and they look at me in horror. They can't understand that I had to follow orders or be put in jail for disobeying direct commands. I did what I thought I had to do to serve my country. 'You killed kids?' they would ask me over and over. 'Why?' I couldn't answer the why, except 'it was necessary.' Was it necessary? Was it really necessary to kill those children and women? After all these years I'm still searching for an answer to that question.

"In nineteen eighty-six I was questioned about and later arrested for the murder of a ten-year-old girl. She was supposedly killed in nineteen seventy-nine.

"My time spent in the county jail awaiting trial was hell due to the fact that a young girl was involved. I was beaten twice by inmates and harassed by jail deputies. The pressure of it all finally got to me, and I attempted suicide. Fortunately, fellow inmates in nearby cells alerted the jail deputies. Shortly afterwards I found Jesus Christ. I had no one else to turn to. My mother wanted to help me but couldn't. I went to trial in nineteen eighty-seven and was given the death sentence. I still had nightmares. I dreamed of Vietnam and what I had witnessed there. I couldn't get away from it; it was everywhere.

"During my trial, evidence was uncovered that another man was questioned and almost charged for the murder I had been convicted of. The man himself admitted that he might have killed the little girl. He couldn't remember. The District Attorney argued that because of my traumatic childhood and my experiences in Vietnam, I had killed a young girl out of frustration and to satisfy my sexual perversions.

"It's extremely difficult to accept my conviction and death sentence. Right up until the guilty verdict was announced, my attorney and I were confident of a not guilty verdict. We were shocked when the verdict was announced. One day, by the grace of God, I'll leave this prison. I will come back — not as an inmate, but as one who cares for those who have become victims of our unjust justice system.

"I'm not bitter, however. I may die for a murder I did not commit, but then again, it may be my just punishment for all those innocent faces. Maybe then I'll be released from my guilt."

John Lohman

U.S. Army

"I joined the Army and went to boot camp in Fort Dix. I was surprised at the number of young men there. It seemed as if the average age was nineteen. Once my training was over, I was given orders to ship out. We were to board the plane that night for Vietnam with only one stop at Anchorage, Alaska, for fuel.

"I was only eighteen and scared as hell. I imagine a lot of us were, but I didn't want to show my fear. None of us could. I decided that I would isolate myself and show no emotions. The older ones reassured us that the airport we'd be landing in at Vietnam was safe. No one aboard had a weapon, and we were told that we'd get our combat gear when we arrived at our permanent duty station.

"As I sat talking to one of the other guys named Bob, I found out he had lied about his age and was only seventeen years old. It made me feel better to know I wasn't the youngest one there. I knew Bob and I would become good friends.

"The landing was smooth, but as we were getting into formation, shots rang out. I didn't realize what they were until I looked around and saw everyone lying on the ground hiding behind their duffel bags. Before I could get down, the boy I had been sitting with and talking to fell in my arms. I thought he had fainted at first, but when I looked down at him, I saw his eyes wide open staring into space. Blood was spilling out from a wound in his forehead all over my uniform, and I panicked. I wanted to run, but there was no place to go.

"All the training I'd had hadn't prepared me for this. The only friend I had in this country lay dead in my arms. I put my hand over the hole trying to stop the bleeding, but it was useless. It never occurred to me that I was making a good target sitting up like I was. I didn't care. I heard voices yelling at me to lie down, but I was in a state of shock. I couldn't seem to move. When the firing stopped, the captain came over and pried my hands off Bob's head. He told me Bob was dead the instant the bullet hit him. There wasn't anything else we could do for him. Bob was going home, in a green body bag. Seventeen years old and life was over for him. I wondered if I would also go home in a green body bag. I felt tears stinging my eyes and angrily brushed them away. I decided to avoid making friends here since they would only die.

I wrote to my girlfriend Marty that night and told her what had happened. I needed someone to talk to. I needed to tell someone how I felt, the fear I felt. I spent the rest of the night in a dirty barracks. Some of the men went to the club for a few drinks and to have a good time. They thought they'd forget the war if they got drunk enough, but I knew it would only be worse in the morning. I couldn't get the sight of Bob's face out of my mind, and it was so hot and humid that I couldn't seem to get any sleep.

"The next morning we were on the back of a truck driving down the only road there. It was paved but had so many holes that it seemed to shake my teeth. I hoped it wasn't going to be a long drive.

"On each side of the road were four-foot drop offs, with rice paddies in the distance. Suddenly I heard gunfire. We were in the middle of an ambush, and none of us had weapons. There were eight regulars there that had M-16s, and the jeep we were in had an M-60 machine gun mounted on it. I ducked for cover and saw that two of the regulars had been wounded. The replacements took cover under the trucks, feeling helpless to do anything but watch.

"The attack was coming from the trees on the other side of the rice paddies and didn't seem to be diminishing. Mike, another replacement, and I grabbed weapons off the wounded and started to return the fire. It was at this moment that we realized the M-60 was quiet. The man that had been firing it had been killed. We ran to the jeep and pushed the body off the gun. We didn't have time to think or to be gentle with the soldier because the firing was coming in faster and faster. The noise was deafening, and we began to fire back. Mike took over the firing while I fed him the ammunition. I fired the M-16 whenever possible and noticed the radio lying on the seat. I picked it up and called for help. The commander yelled our location to me, and I told them we needed some artillery fire on the mortar location. It wasn't long before the mortar was knocked out of the battle and the others fled. We had lost one man, had two wounded and had picked up four prisoners. This was only the beginning. I felt pride and whispered that this one was for Bob.

"I arrived at Phu Loi with no further incidents. As I looked around, I noticed how awful it looked. At least we had running water which was often unheard of. They were using outhouses with fifty-five gallon drums

John Lohman

cut in half and placed inside under the opening. The smell was terrible. The place was called sand bag city. There were a few wooden buildings, but most of the camp was covered with tents. All structures were surrounded by three foot stacks of sand bags. The TOC (Tactical Operation Center) was at least fifteen feet tall. The sand bags not only went the entire height of the walls but also covered the roof.

"I was assigned the job of chart operator. I was to take the information that came from the unit in the field and plot the distance and angle of fire from our guns to the target. The most disagreeable part of the job was the fact that we worked eight hours then were off eight hours. Our bodies never got used to when we should sleep or when we should work.

"One night we were watching an out-of-door movie similar to the drive-in movies at home. The bunkers started firing their weapons, and we took cover. The fight only lasted twenty minutes, and when it was over twenty-four Cong were dead. Opening fire, I managed to hit one of them and as I crept closer, I could see the young face of a boy of ten or eleven years old. Blood was trickling down his face, and his eyes were wide open. I fell to my knees and threw up. Beside the boy's body was a satchel charge he was to throw but he never had a chance. He would have killed the whole lot of us had he been able to get it off. I had killed him first. I felt revulsion that I'd had to kill so young a child, but it had been him or us.

"I could hear the sucking sound of mud and water in my combat boots as we walked through the rice paddies. We were going slow, not knowing where the VC were hiding. You never saw these people; they blended into the countryside. I thought more of Bob and how he'd died as time went on. I listened to the body counts they gave us credit for after each fire mission. I wanted more bodies, more kills. I hated prisoners.

"I wrote to Marty everyday but never received an answer. My letters were always returned, and I felt bitter. I had to keep writing to keep my sanity even though it appeared she had deserted me. I felt sure her parents had intercepted the mail and had them returned to me. They had never liked me and didn't want their daughter involved with someone who was fighting in the war.

"The fighting stayed pretty much the same for the rest of my tour. There was no real break day in and day out, and I wondered if it would ever end. The country itself was pretty, and I thought if they took away the barbwire and the soldiers that it would be beautiful. The flatlands were filled with rice paddies. They would farm them during the day and fight us at night. It was difficult to tell the farmer from the Viet Cong. They both wore black pajamas.

"There was another type of people in the mountains that we found we

35

could trust more than the others. They had strange customs though. If the village chief liked you, he would offer you a woman for the night. The only way you could refuse without insulting them was to say that you were Catholic or married.

"Between the rice paddies and the mountains you find the villages and the jungle. We had to learn early in our patrols that there is no such thing as a friendly village. There were times when the jungle was more friendly than the village. In the villages you found girls of twelve selling themselves. The going rate for a girl was one dollar. You could buy anything you wanted in the village, hashish, marijuana or even opium. Your dollar would buy anything you wanted.

"There were horrors such as malaria, punji stakes, NVR, Cong, and Bengal tigers, not to mention smaller things such as infection. The jungle takes care of its own though and we found out we could take the leeches that were sucking blood from us and place them on the infected area and they would suck the infection out.

"When I first came to Vietnam I was eighteen, and a year later I felt like I was forty-five. You do a lot of growing up over there. I never got used to seeing these people live in their unsanitary conditions doing things that no American would do in our lowest class slum areas. They would wash their clothing in the water where, just a short distance upstream, someone would be using as a bathroom. Not only was the laundry done there, but they would bring the clothes to wash, and bathe their bodies when they thought of it. Most of them looked like they never washed, and if you got close to them the odor was terrible.

"The fields in Vietnam were fertilized with raw waste products from animals, but the use of human waste materials was a common practice. Whenever they needed to relieve themselves, they would do it in the middle of the street, anywhere they happened to be. They had no running water as we know it. Most of the water would have to be brought from the streams in buckets.

"As a Vietnamese citizen you could smoke opium, use it, deal in it, or whatever you wanted to do. Drugs were no big deal over there, and it was sold to the Americans cheaply. The Army finally had to make it a crime for a villager to sell drugs to the servicemen. Unfortunately, this didn't stop it from happening. They had no respect for human life other than for their own. The Vietnamese had no loyalties. You would fight side by side with them, and when it looked like the other side was winning, they would cross over and join them.

"Soon my time was down to nine days, and I'd be able to go home. I felt apprehension and fear that I might be killed before I could go home.

John Lohman

I had managed to save some money while in Vietnam, and I bought some items to take home to my family. The prices were cheap, and I was able to buy lots of pretty things to take back to the States. I had thought a lot about life since being in 'Nam and was glad to be going home. I would spend the first two weeks with my sister in California and try to get my life in order again. It would feel good to take a hot bath and sleep between sheets again. There would be no more months of rain. The sound from the constant firing of weapons would be gone.

"I boarded the plane that was to take us home. It was full of servicemen just as anxious as I was to leave this country that only brought pain and death. Everyone was silent until the pilot got on the intercom and announced that we were no longer in Vietnam. A loud cheer went out from all on board, and the stewardess brought out drinks for everyone. To some of us, she was the first woman with round eyes we had seen in a year. Fashion had changed a lot and we appreciated the short skirts they were now wearing. I didn't know just how much things had changed in the States. I didn't know I was going home to be ridiculed and yelled at.

"Even as I was heading for home, I thought of Bob and felt sorrow. I remembered the body bags we were carrying in the cargo compartment of the plane. Along with the sorrow, I felt guilt. Why should I be allowed to come home when other soldiers lay in the cold compartment, dead?

"When we landed, I was surprised to find the American public didn't hail us as heroes. There were people at the airport who yelled obscene things at us as we walked from the plane. They were demonstrating against the war in Vietnam. They continually threw things at us. We were called baby killers and worse. I was spit at, cursed and called names. I was frustrated and angry that I had risked my life to fight for freedom, and this was my homecoming.

Feelings are sometimes hard to control, especially if these feelings have been kept buried deep inside you for a long time. Mine were hidden from everyone, including myself.

"My sister took me to her home, and for the first time in a year I had a real bath. The wonderful tan I thought I had all washed down the drain. It was dirt. She had fixed dinner for me and her two daughters and it was wonderful. Dinner was fried chicken and baked potatoes with tossed salad topped off with a glass of wine. I had dreamed of such a meal for over a year as I ate C-rations. Never had anything tasted so good before. It seemed like I had been gone for many years instead of just one.

"She never brought up the subject of the war. I guess she thought I didn't want to talk about it. I had thought I was close enough to my sister to talk to her about anything, but I found I couldn't talk of the war. I felt the need to shut her out of that part of my life. She didn't understand my feelings."

Eugene "Red" McDaniel

U.S. Naval Pilot

Red was 35 years old, with light brown hair that had enough red in it to get his nickname "Red." He was a military veteran and had served his country for many years. His body still looked lean and hard from exercising and hard work.

He was told he had to go on a mission, an alpha strike against the strategic truck repair center. It was a dangerous mission and Red felt a flutter of doubt go through him. He had a beautiful wife and three children who lived in Virginia Beach, Virginia. How he wanted to be home with them instead of going on this mission. It was his 81st mission, and he felt that maybe death awaited him. It was just a nagging thought, but it kept coming back to haunt him. He'd never felt this fear during the other missions and hoped that it would disappear.

Kelly Patterson was his bombardier-navigator that morning, and soon they were above the clouds heading for their mission when they saw SAM missiles looming up in front of them. A violent explosion jarred the plane, sending them into a dive. They knew they would have to bail out before the bomb load blew them out of the sky.

Kelly was the first to shoot out, then Red. As he floated down onto enemy territory, Red felt like a puppet. He could see Kelly's parachute far in the horizon. The smoke from the plane was a signal to the Vietnamese that an American pilot had gone down.

Red's parachute landed in the trees, and when he jumped the 40 feet to the ground he hurt his back. He didn't know it then, but he had crushed two vertebra. For a few minutes he just lay there on the ground, too stunned to move. After a few minutes he forced himself to get up, knowing it wouldn't take the enemy long to locate where he had gone down.

Using the survival radio, he made contact and said he had an injured back but that he would make it all right. As time went on, he began to pray, reminding God that he was a good Baptist. He prayed for the Jolly

Green Giants to come in time to rescue him before the Viet Cong could find him.

The next morning he heard a rifle fire and looked up to see 15 Vietnamese peasants around him. He felt fear and knew he couldn't run; he'd never make it. They tied his arms behind hid back and led him away through the jungle. He had been stripsearched, and he was put in a small room. By this time his arms and legs had begun to swell, and he couldn't feel them. After awhile he was taken again on a journey to Hanoi. As he marched, the Vietnamese would hit him with their rifle butts and kick his legs. They'd slap him and laugh at his discomfort as he struggled to stay on his feet.

Red was taken to the "Hanoi Hilton," the main American prison camp. He was taken to a small windowless room which smelled like mold and mildew. The iron gates clanged shut behind him, and he tried to lie down to get some sleep. He was exhausted by this time and just wanted to sleep. This was not to be though, because in a few minutes, a Vietnamese officer came in and read him the camp regulations. He told Red that he was not to talk to any other prisoners, or he'd be sorry. Red felt better just knowing there were other Americans there with him. He thought he might get to see his old friends who had been shot down earlier. He was taken to the interrogators who tried to get him to talk about his military information. He refused to talk to them except to give his name, serial number and rank. This made them angry, and they tied him up with very tight ropes.

He wouldn't answer any of the questions and the pain became more intense. They would loosen the ropes for a few minutes, then they would put them back on tighter than ever. He had to go to the bathroom but wasn't allowed to go. Finally he lost control and felt the warm urine running down his pant legs. The pain was getting worse, and he decided that he would tell them something that didn't matter just so they would let him free. It would have to be phony, but he just had to do something to get relief.

For the next few days he fed them phony information and was let out of the irons and ropes and taken to an area that was called the wash area. There, other prisoners washed up and cleaned their clothes when they were allowed to.

He wondered if he could go through that kind of torture many more times and still refuse to answer the questions. He could hear the screams of other prisoners as they were being tortured and knew they were going through the same things that he himself had gone through. He had to find a way to talk to the other prisoners, but the Vietnamese were ensuring that no one talked while in the wash area. They knew that the men could take more pain if they were linked together with their own kind.

From Vietnam to Hell

They had a camp code that they used to communicate with each other. He would have to learn the code. The loneliness was unbearable, and the Vietnamese knew they could break the men's spirits if they could keep them separated from each other.

The men would tap out messages to one another through the wall and would know what was going on. They became very close and would give moral support to each other, especially during times of torture. The soup they lived on was poor, but it kept them alive. Some of the men would eat caterpillars and bugs they caught in the cells. One night Red heard a man coughing all through the night. When they checked on him, they found a tapeworm trying to get up through his throat. This was a common problem in Vietnam, and many of the men would have them.

The years dragged on with them being taken out one by one to be tortured for days on end. Some of the men didn't live through the torture sessions, and you could hear the screams of the dying men. The Vietnamese took great pleasure in inflicting pain on Americans. They would laugh as they inflicted the most brutal types of torture. Two men escaped from the prison, and it put the Viet Cong in a rage. Vowing to find out who was responsible, they took the men one by one to the torture chambers. Red knew it was only a matter of time before they came to get him. He was taken to the torture chambers and put in leg irons. They put his arms behind his back in wrist irons and pulled tighter and tighter. He was made to drop his pants and, with a rubber belt, was whipped on his buttocks. He lost count of the times. They would stop just long enough to ask who was responsible for the escape. When Red wouldn't tell them what they wanted to hear, they continued. He was made to sit upright with his arms around his head and told to stay that way. If he dropped his arms even an inch, they would beat him again. This went on for days, and he tried to pray for strength. He needed strength to keep on living, to return to his family. The pain was excruciating and never seemed to let up. He began to get infections all over the cuts on his body, and the pus oozed down his legs. He began to have hallucinations and didn't know where he was.

The questions went on, but Red wouldn't tell on the committee. He would not tell on his fellow men. He felt he had to protect them. His captors were getting madder because he wouldn't talk. They put him in the ropes again, and this time they tossed the rope over a ceiling beam and ran it through a pulley. Then they pulled him off the ground, and he was left dangling in the air. The pain was worse than any he had experienced up till then, and he heard his bone crack.

Still Red hung on, never telling the Cong what they wanted to hear. His strength and determination were miraculous; they didn't know

40

how to break this man. They gave him electric shocks on and off, and the pain was unbearable; still he hung on.

They promised to stop the torture if he would talk. That was all he had to do: tell who the escape committee was. He heard their voices as if from a long way off, but he still stood his ground. Finally after many days of torture, they cut him loose. He had lost control of his hands because the ropes had damaged the nerves, but he was still alive.

They took him to the wash area so he could clean the waste and blood off himself. He had to let the water run over him because he couldn't use his hands to wash off. Then he was taken back in and put in leg irons again. They took turns beating him with the rubber hose. Finally Red told them that he was the committee. They accepted this and stopped.

He was taken to a cell with Lieutenant Commander Windy Rivers. He looked at Red as if he were a dead man. He began to do what he could for him, washing his body, feeding and shaving him.

He slowly got better, and in 1970 they moved the men up to a new compound called Camp Faith. They were allowed to talk to each other in this camp, and Red knew the end of the war must be near. Now they were given bread along with their soup, and they were able to boil water to make coffee.

After being a POW for six years, Red was told they were going home. They were taken by bus and put on a plane where they were taken to Clark Air Force Base. There were reporters, and the men shook hands with the welcoming committee.

From there, Red was taken to see his family. The children had grown so much during the six years he'd been away, and he felt such love at seeing them again. He held tightly to his wife and knew she had spent many hours with other POW wives in helping to free the men. Then suddenly he was home, and he looked around at all the familiar things that were so dear to him.

He realized that it was his faith that had brought him home safely from the hell of being a prisoner of war. He remembered Kelly who did not come and hoped he had died instantly instead of being tortured until death finally overcame him.

Red was assigned duty on Capitol Hill, to serve as the Navy and Marine Corps liaison to the House of Representatives. His country told him that all the living POWs had come home during the "Big Release" of 1973. But still he wondered if they really had. Were some of them still alive in Vietnam waiting for their country to rescue them? The question began to haunt him. He had nightmares. Were men like Kelly still struggling to survive their captivity in bamboo cages and prison cells somewhere in Indochina?

From Vietnam to Hell

Most of the men who came back have suffered from PTSD in one way or another. Sometimes it took years to find out just what the problem was.

"I'm not sure at what moment I learned the truth about America's handling of information concerning Americans still missing," Red stated. "At what point in freedom did I cross the line from questioning my country's integrity to the absolute certainty that America knowingly left some men behind? I'm not sure. I am sure that I could have been one of them."

"For me the Vietnam War is not over. It won't end until we bring home those men who were left behind. The ordeal won't end until my questions about my country's honor are answered. America has forsaken some of her bravest men. Worse than that, America has forsaken some of her highest ideals: liberty, justice, loyalty, righteousness. These same ideals kept me going from day to day in my captivity. They are the ideals that keep me going from day to day now in my search for answers to some deeply disturbing questions about my country. As the American people become aware of the tragedy of the men still held captive by the communists in Southeast Asia, I believe there will be a national outcry to bring them home. I pray that it will not be too late."

Red McDaniel received the Navy's highest award for bravery, the Navy Cross. His many other military decorations include two Silver Stars, two Legions of Merit with combat "V" (for combat valor), two Distinguished Flying Crosses, three Bronze Stars with combat "V" and two Purple Hearts for wounds resulting from the torture he endured as a POW. Red continues to work on Capitol Hill as president and founder of the American Defense Foundation.

Chuck Dean
U.S. Army

"When I was a young paratrooper, going through jungle training and various schools to acclimate my still-forming mind into the war mentality, I dreamed of going to war, winning medals and protecting our country from evil-intending invading hordes. Spit-shined jumpboots, sparkling brass and to the skin haircuts were my order of the day. I was enthusiastic, and Vietnam gave me the opportunity to join the ranks of heroes who had gone to war in years past.

"Upon graduation from jump school, I was assigned to the 82nd Airborne Division at Fort Bragg, North Carolina. I was restless. The Cuba invasion at the Bay of Pigs was long gone, and I wanted to see some action. I wanted to win some medals, but there was no war. Life lingered on pulling guard duty, KP, with senseless inspections and drunken nights in Fayetteville.

"One day I met a new man who had just arrived from duty in Okinawa. He said he was sent over to a place called Vietnam to be a door gunner on a helicopter for thirty days. He described life on Okinawa as having no guard duty, no KP and providing a chance to get involved in a war and get combat decorations without the long-term commitment to the drudgery of war. It looked good to me, so I found myself in front of the career counselor the next day, reenlisting for an extra year so I could go to Okinawa.

"In May of nineteen sixty-five, President Johnson ordered us onto C-130 aircraft. We were deployed into South Vietnam as the first regular combat unit to enter the war. We were told that we would be in South Vietnam for a temporary duty assignment of sixty days. We were to sweep into areas where no free forces had ever gone, secure them, turn them over to the control of the South Vietnamese Army, and return to Okinawa. We were excited. Here was our chance to do a little fighting, win a few medals and then return safely. But it didn't work that way.

43

From Vietnam to Hell

"After our temporary duty, we were extended indefinitely to South Vietnam. Other Army divisions and units began to arrive, and we knew that the good life was over. The little bit of jungle rot, malaria and rotten conditions were going to be with us for a long time. Our 'temporary' assignment was the first of many lies to come from our government.

"I was in the advanced party of the first U.S. ground troops to launch offensive operations in South Vietnam in nineteen sixty-five. My brigade entered the war with a naïveté inspired by John Wayne movies and war stories from Dad or big brother in the big war, World War II. We wanted very much to come home in glory and be welcomed into the folds of America's honored warriors. Like so many other dreams we had, that never happened. The bubble began to burst when we started to get reports that our own people back home didn't want us to fight anymore.

"In our training on Okinawa, the Philippines, Taiwan and Irimote, we were prepared to kill people who were identified as enemies. To accomplish this, the Army employed several psychological tactics. First, they made the enemy less than human to us. 'Gooks, dinks and zipperheads' were born in our minds and vocabulary. We were convinced that the enemy was a bunch of soulless heathens, godless creatures that mutilate and destroy, who needed to be dealt with as a menace to the world.

"I remember one time we had just come back from an operation. Things were lax. There was a kid who came around selling rice, wine and sugar cane. He was about twelve or so. I could never tell how old those people were, but he wasn't very old. His bicycle was booby-trapped and suddenly exploded in our midst. We lost about eight guys there. The worst part of it was that I had to shoot the kid as he was running away, and it was my first kill. If I close my eyes right now, I can be there. I didn't want to blow him away, you know. I said, 'God . . . let me hit him where he won't get hurt.' I just wanted to stop him — but what's the use of stopping him? So, for some reason I aimed my rifle at the base of his neck, where I could hit him right in the head. It seems that I held it for hours and hours; it took forever to pull the trigger. But I know it was only a few seconds. It all flashed in front of me in slow motion; the bullet making impact and him rolling over, becoming a dead heap in the middle of the road. Now I'll be driving a car, I'll see a little kid, and I imagine. . . .

"Vietnam was a different kind of war. At the time we didn't know it. I remember one day when a four-year-old wandered into a crowd of soldiers to beg for food. His eyes sparkled when we gave him something to eat. Then he exploded into pieces from the satchel charge he never knew was on his back. Booby-trapping innocent children didn't seem like the way war was supposed to be fought.

Chuck Dean

"My unit, the 173rd Airborne Brigade, was one of a kind in the military history of this country. It was the only military unit that never set foot on American soil. The Brigade was formed on Okinawa and retired in Vietnam at the end of the war. Since we were the reactionary force for Asia, we were the first to go to Vietnam in nineteen sixty-five. The 173rd was designed to be very mobile. Therefore, every trooper was a combatant, regardless of whether he was a typist, mechanic or cook. When the unit went into action, everybody was on the line. There was no carpet that you could crawl under, no safe air-conditioned rear area.

"At the peak of America's involvement, the total number of troops committed to Vietnam was five hundred thousand. Fewer than fifty thousand were engaged in fighting in the field; four hundred fifty thousand men and women were in the security defense of these big bases. We didn't lose the war because we were poor soldiers in the field. We lost because so few of us actually got in there to do what we were trained to do.

"It was two o'clock in the morning, and the temperature was still hovering around ninety degrees. We had turned in our weapons and gear the previous day and were confined to this tiny barbwire compound on Ton Sanh Nhut Airbase for a day and a half. After thirty cans of beer each, the thirty or so troopers crowded into the little space and scrounged for a place to sleep.

"Our plane, a commercial jet airliner, would be arriving and leaving in four hours. We were going back to the world. Our war was over, and now everything would be made right again. Home was only a few hours away.

"I had managed to find a mattress inside the semblance of a building, corrugated tin and scrap wood thrown together. I was on the brink of slipping into a drunken stupor when the frightening concussion of mortar explosions knocked me to the ground. I instinctively threw the mattress over me as the airbursting explosions ripped through the tiny compound. At first I pounded my fists into the ground in anger as I yelled out, 'You're not going to get me now, Charlie!' And then I broke. I sobbed out to God, 'Oh God, I've been through too much to get taken out now. Just let me go home. Please.'

"As suddenly as it had begun, the explosions ceased. My thoughts of God vanished in the confusion, heightened by the drunken condition of everyone in the compound. I heard the wounded crying out and someone vainly screaming to his dead friend to get up.

"Seven teenage soldiers died that morning in a tiny compound halfway around the world. After spending a year in hell, this was their reward. How unjust it seemed. But after coming home and seeing how we were received by the people who had sent us to fight, I thought that they were the lucky ones. They escaped the war after Vietnam; we did not.

"Eighteen hours later, I found myself in a mystical, dreamlike place called San Francisco International Airport. As I walked through the crowd, I was amazed. There were clean people, and the perfume and cologne were nearly overwhelming to a nose that for two years had only smelled decaying flesh, human waste, gun powder and pungent Asian food. These people didn't seem to know a war was going on, and I felt myself beginning to lose my bearings. A deep confusion set in. All my childhood dreams of being a war hero with a grateful country cheering me on blew up in my mind. I was not only ignored, but had become an outcast from the very people who had sent me.

"I found that the only time I could put up with people was when I was drunk. When that didn't work, I isolated myself and smoked marijuana until I became unconscious. I found myself sleeping with a K-bar under my pillow. I had loaded weapons around my bedroom and all over the house. I felt it was absolutely necessary. It was the sort of thing one lived with. I went through situations where I ended up pulling these weapons on people because I was startled in the night.

"Vietnam is like a cancer in all of us. It quietly eats us up after a while. We can only stuff those experiences inside us for so long before they begin to eat their way to the surface. I'd like to talk to someone about these things, but I don't think there's anyone interested in talking about hell. For us the war never ended. But no one in 'the world' can see that but us, and that is the biggest letdown of all. We struggled hard to survive 'Nam so we could come back into the world we knew and loved. Then we found out that the world didn't want to hear about 'Nam or have anything to do with our problems. Home, the place we thought would be our heaven, had become our hell.

"Three months later I entered another Army recruiting station to re-up for another hitch. I couldn't relate to anyone at home. I thought I could find some peace with living in America by using the Army as a means to help me readjust.

"I was assigned to Fort Ord, California, and my work would be guarding prisoners in the stockade. The last thing I needed was to follow a bunch of American prisoners around with a shotgun while they cleaned up trash. I told the first sergeant that I didn't trust myself with loaded weapons. I felt I would have killed them if they so much as looked cross-eyed at me. They decided another assignment might be best in my case. I was to become a drill instructor for basic training troops.

"My next two years were a maze of conflicts, doubts and further alienation. Every trainee became a little green machine, a number that looked exactly like the one standing beside it or in rank behind it. I avoided personal relationships with these young men. Old fears arose, of getting too close to someone and then having him get killed or wounded. Consequently, I didn't want to know anything about the hundreds of teenagers whom I was sending to a distant land of terror, drugs and pain.

"During this time I was spending my off hours with some hippie friends. We talked philosophy, smoked pot, and shared free sex. My hair grew longer and my mustache was completely against Army regulations. After a year and a half of this duty, I met a young woman and we were married. It was at this point that I was introduced to LSD, and my bride and I were high on acid every weekend from that point forward. Something happened to my mind under the influence of that very potent drug, and it became obvious to my superiors at the post. I was assigned to the John F. Kennedy Special Forces Center, where I would be trained in Vietnamese language and 'other' training. This could only mean one thing—I was on my way back to 'Nam, even though I had been guaranteed I would not return there.

"We were going back to Vietnam as CIA operatives to do some very ugly things to the Vietnamese and Americans. I made my decision right then that I would not go. With my new hippie wife, I would leave the Army and America before I would go back to murder people for the CIA. This we did. I couldn't imagine myself going AWOL. My wife and I hooked up with many underground anti-war groups and used an underground railroad to get to Canada. Our drug usage increased, and we moved from one hippie commune to the next. Our lives were shattered. Our beautiful world of sexual anything goes, laced with psychedelic drugs, brought on some of my life's deepest depressions. With so little to dream about or hope for, we were committing a slow form of suicide.

"After more than six years of hell, I went to the Vancouver Airport and turned myself over to U.S. Immigration authorities. Life wasn't working. I was sent to Fort Benjamin Harrison, Indiana, where I was mustered out of the Army with an undesirable discharge. President Ford offered me amnesty if I would participate in the alternate service program. After completing my work assignments, my discharge was upgraded to a general discharge under honorable conditions.

"My wife finally agreed to a divorce after thirteen years. My PTSD reaction of not allowing people to be close or to care for me was obviously out of control again. I erased my second wife from my life with a good Mexican lawyer and a hundred dollar bill.

"Then a miracle happened to me. A friend introduced me to a friend of

From Vietnam to Hell

Chuck Dean

hers. What a different person she was—strong, self-reliant and beautiful. She was a successful business owner with so much class that she scared me. We began dating, and I fell in love. Athena became Mrs. Charles Dean on Valentine's Day, barely two months after we'd met. My wandering eyes and lust for other women ended as abruptly as a sudden-death game. After a couple of months, I told her I had been to Vietnam. When she began to see the stress reemerging in my life, she became concerned. She recognized that the man she had married had been deeply hurt and his pain was beginning to affect the marriage. Every time we went to a party, I would overdo the drinking and drugs. My wild, drunken streaks of loud, boisterous fun were not fun to her. Our marriage took on a different tone when I began to show disinterest in the business and to step back and do other things that weren't related to it, including more writing, painting and fundraising. But it wasn't until we received a promotion and moved to Seattle that things became really bad.

"I went off the deep end when I got together with an old friend, a Vietnam veteran. He was involved with an organization that protested taxes and radically opposed the current government structure, and I soon became a fanatic.

"During the course of a year, Athena threatened to kick me out. She told me that it was all over, that she wanted a divorce. This devastated me.

I knew she had caused so many positive changes in me, and I was committing another relational suicide with the best woman in the world. After a week I broke down and called a friend in Burbank. Bill was in the same business as Athena and had helped us many times before. I told him I needed a friend. He told me I needed the Lord. I straightened up in the chair and wiped my nose and brushed the tears from my red, swollen eyes. I agreed to pray with him and give my heart and soul to Jesus. When I got off the phone, I didn't hear angels singing or rockets going off, but I felt a peace that I hadn't felt before. Athena found out that I had called Bill, and she called him to find out what was going on. She had never had much exposure to God or the church. Her father was a professing atheist, and she grew up with virtually no religious background. Athena soon forgave me, and we were restored as husband and wife, all the divorce plans whisked away forever. Three weeks later, Athena asked the Lord to forgive her and enter her life. Seeing her transformed as I had been added to the miracle that had happened in my life.

"My urge to drink and use drugs vanished abruptly. The heavy symptoms of my PTSD felt like part of another life that I had once lived, but was now dead and gone. The nightmares and horrible mental pictures of the war had been transferred from my present self to the former Chuck, the dead person who was no longer part of my life. It was as if Jesus had taken all the mental images from my subconscious mind and mounted them in a photo album. I could still see them from time to time, but they no longer impinged on my life or dictated the symptoms of post-traumatic stress disorder. I had finally found peace for my troubled mind.

"The repressed trauma of Vietnam ended for me, but I soon found that the price of God's gift of freedom is a new battle. Because I know him, I now carry the burden to help others battle with their memories of the war. Many soldiers claim that in basic training they were taught how to be animals. They take you down, tear you apart and put you back together again piece by piece . . . the way they want you to be. You are taught not to think, but to react. You are taught to be an animal. Then you're expected to suddenly forget your training as an animal after the war. . . . You know how to act like an animal. You don't know how to be a human being anymore.'

"Our training began the process of dehumanizing us. It removed God's basic gifts to us — love and caring for others. First we lost our trust in emotions, replacing it with repressed rage and social isolation. Trained to take life, we reentered a society whose foundation was 'Thou shalt not kill.' We all went to Vietnam with some degree of faith, based on either our beliefs or on the Christian principles and morality upon which our country was founded. Many of us lost our faith because we felt we had been had by

From Vietnam to Hell

God, our country and our leaders. We felt that God was somewhere else while we had to witness and be exposed to horrible things. So we blamed Him. I can remember praying during incoming mortar attacks or firefights, and then getting up off the ground afterwards and saying to myself, 'Well, you pulled yourself through another one.' Never once did I give credit to God for having saved my life, even though I had prayed furiously during the heat of danger. And that's the point. God did not go AWOL in Vietnam. Instead, he kept us alive and brought us back for a purpose. But you won't discover that purpose until you make peace with Vietnam and with God. Point Man Ministries can help you do this. Contact one of the outposts, and they will help you take off the rucksack of pain and return to living life as you were meant to. That is my invitation to you, personally. I believe you are now ready to make peace with your past. We'll take the point."

Point Man International
PO Box 440
Mountlake Terrace, WA 98043
(206) 486-5383

Chuck Dean is executive director of Point Man International, a Seattle-based, non-profit veterans-for-veterans support organization dedicated to healing the war wounds of the Vietnam veteran.

Point Man Ministries

Every Vietnam vet knows what a point man is. During a military patrol or infantry operation, the point man walks several meters in front of everyone else. His purpose is to serve as the eyes and ears for the unit following him through suspected enemy territory. He seeks out likely enemy ambush sites, booby traps, and anything else that would endanger or entrap his trailing companions.

Point Man Ministries is designed to do the same for Vietnam veterans through the healing power of the Holy Spirit, the inerrant Word of God, and the cleansing blood of Jesus Christ. It is a ministry run by vets for vets that provides individual and group counseling, literature, and seminars to help bring aid and comfort to their brothers in arms.

Point Man has but one guarantee: If you turn your life over to the Lord Jesus Christ, you will be healed. In 1984, a vision for reaching out to war veterans and their families was given to the late William Landreth, Jr. Bill was an Infantry Platoon Leader serving with the Army's American (23rd infantry) Division, 1968–1969. Lt. Landreth was seriously wounded and retired from the army for medical reasons in 1972.

After military service he earned a degree in psychology. After many personal bouts with post-traumatic stress disorder, he turned to Jesus Christ and found the ultimate healing for his post-war problems. It was at this time that he and his wife, Jan, started Point Man Ministries and officially incorporated it as a Washington State non-profit organization.

Bill suddenly passed away on October 12, 1986, and the ministry was shelved by January. In March of 1987, Jan approached Chuck Dean, a Vietnam veteran who served with the 173rd Airborne, 1964–1966, and asked if he would accept the responsibility for running the ministry. The ministry has continued from the original concept to an unfolding of the complete vision of what God has in store for Vietnam veterans and their families and all the victims of trauma.

Point Man Ministries is comprised of Vietnam veterans from all branches of the armed forces.

"Our technological society of the '80s has forgotten the deaths of more than fifty thousand young men in Southeast Asia. But for many who returned from the hostile jungles of Vietnam so many years ago, the agonizing memories continue to linger on," said Mickey Block of the U.S. Navy SEAL team.

With that statistic in mind, the Point Men of Point Man Ministries have dedicated themselves to the comfort and aid of their brothers in arms. Point Man Ministries provides a support group setting where the veteran can meet with other Vietnam veterans and finally lower his emotional perimeter. It also provides counseling, emergency shelter and other services, all from veterans who have been down the same trails and understand where others are coming from. These services are provided at no charge because Point Man Ministries is a nonprofit organization.

The weekly group meetings emphasize a family atmosphere. They understand that 'Nam vets will open up or accept counseling only from other Vietnam veterans. The brotherhood is based on a shared trauma. Point Man is run solely by Vietnam veterans.

They avoid secular counseling procedures. The sessions are different. Their first concern is to help the veteran develop trust again. They begin each meeting by identifying the members, what unit they were in while in Vietnam, what year they were in Vietnam and what they are doing now. Most veterans have probably not been able to talk with anyone about the war for years. At a Point Man outpost meeting, the vet can sit down with a bunch of guys who are not going to criticize him. He can listen and watch, without being expected to say or do much of anything. In time he will feel relaxed because he will recognize he has finally run into a group of guys who understand and express genuine concern. They won't give up if he explodes in rage, or cries, or walks away. They have been there, too.

Point Men will prod gently to help the vet open up and let go of his memories and pain. The outpost leaders will treat the vet with respect, friendship and love. They rely on God and prayer.

Like physical wounds, psychological and emotional wounds have to be cleaned out before they can heal. People clean these kinds of wounds by letting it out, confessing the pain, hurt, anger, sorrow, terror and remorse. A Point Man outpost meeting provides the safest environment in which to do this. The vet finally can talk about the horrible things he witnessed, did, or failed to stop while in Vietnam. No one will judge him because everyone is there to find healing for himself and to help others in the process. The security of knowing that every man in the group has probably done similar things during the war encourages honesty and trust, maybe for the first time since the war.

Craig McLaren of Bessemen, Alabama, has been appointed to the

Point Man Ministries

office of Director of Incarcerated Veterans by the Board of Directors of Point Man International. Craig served with the 173rd Airborne Brigade during the Vietnam War and is highly decorated. He is also the President of VVA Chapter 190 and serves as an officer in many other service organizations.

One part of the traditional treatment for Vietnam veterans is in a sad situation. Secular counseling has pronounced PTSD as an incurable commodity vets earned for serving their country as they did. In fact, some PTSD problems are considered untreatable in many vets.

Vietnam veterans are not the only victims of the war. Their families likewise suffer from the effects of PTSD. The emotional numbing, depression and alienation that have isolated the veteran from his family are symptoms of his post-traumatic stress from the war. These are very obvious. But the psychological wounds within the family are not as readily perceived.

Research clearly indicates that veteran families are affected both emotionally and spiritually by the veteran's stress. To help himself, he must help his family. They need to have a deep understanding of things that cause or trigger his reactions.

The most difficult thing for family members to do is to keep from taking any attack of anger or hostility as a personal affront. Often the anger and attacks are directed at the veteran himself, or the government, the no-win syndrome of Vietnam, or his inability to be in control of events around him. It is frightening for a veteran's family to live with his unpredictable emotions on a daily basis.

It was about a year ago that Chuck and Athena Dean began to see the need for a ministry directed specifically to the needs of the family members of veterans. The divorce rate for Vietnam veterans is near an incredible 90 percent, and most are in their second or third marriage. Family members are often more receptive to ministry than the veterans themselves. Project Homefront can help families understand the reasons behind the emotional problems that veterans manifest. There are 42 local chapters of Project Homefront to date.

Sgt. Jake

U.S. Army

"I went in the Army in my senior year of high school. I went to the Alaskan National Guard. A year later I was married and had one child when President Johnson activated all combat National Guard, and I was called to go. It was a bitter pill to take because I was settled with a steady job, a wife and a six-month-old child.

"My wife and I sat down and talked about it. My father and I didn't talk very much; he was a World War II veteran. Every male child in our family had always served when there was a war. My father thought the National Guard was a copout. We argued over it, but it was what I had chosen to do and I did it.

"When the activation came, all he said about it was that it would give me a chance to serve my country. I stood up and took the oath; I gave my word on it. I didn't really think it was fair that they'd activated me, but it had always been a possibility. No one had lied and said we wouldn't go.

"I was given an additional six months training where I qualified for Special Forces. I was being trained in Germany and didn't have any fear of going to Vietnam. On December third, nineteen sixty-seven, I was told to pack my bags. Something told me that I was going to Vietnam, and four hours later I was put aboard a plane and sent to Turkey.

"We were issued jungle warfare gear. The American Liaison Team put us through our paces and on December twenty-second, we were airlifted to Vietnam. We took fire coming in, and, although we were trained combat men, nothing prepared us for what was to happen next. When we hit the ground, the North Vietnamese Army was in the compound, and we went at it nose to nose right from the opener. Ten minutes later it was all over. They had never experienced this; it was the first airdrop the U.S. made in South Vietnam.

"I was greatly shaken but still excited. I was young and the idea of actually being there weighed heavily on my mind. I couldn't believe that this

54

was actually happening to me, and I'm proud to say this excitement stayed with me the whole time I was over there.

"I was sent from there to Bravo Company, 39th engineers at Chu Lai. My first six months were spent in the construction business. We took fire and rocket attacks and participated in the evacuation of different personnel. We provided security for the teams in there. We thought that Chu Lai would be the biggest installation in East Asia, which it eventually became.

"I wound up with the 198th Infantry doing security patrol. We were involved in the only armored attack by the North Vietnamese in the whole conflict. We eventually stopped five tanks with hand grenades and .45s. They pinned us down in the bunkers, and we withstood the rifle fire for about nine hours. We had ninety refugee children with us, and we tried to get them out. The enemy started firing into those children. I was with them because I was part of the security team that was taking them out.

"We were running, dragging those kids with us as fast as we could go, and when we hit the tree line, the North Vietnamese Army was there. It became extremely violent for a while. Most of us were wounded, and we were cut off from returning to the compound. We were alone in the woods with these children. I radioed for help, and they promised to pick us up but didn't. Five days later, I, along with four other men who had survived, made it to the river. We had nineteen children with us. I never knew what happened to the rest of them who hadn't been killed in the first attack.

"At that time it became personal. I was no longer an objective observer. I took it upon myself to try to kill every gook in the world. I wanted to kill them all, not some of them, but every one. For the next twenty-seven months, I walked the point.

"I participated in one hundred twenty-one air missions and was involved in seven major conflicts including Hamburger Hill. I was finally injured in May of nineteen seventy. I spent eighteen months in the hospital. I had an arm cut off, and was shot in the knee, head, and back.

"I came home in nineteen seventy. I didn't pay attention to where I was. My marriage ended, and I was alone. I had inherited a lot of money from my grandfather, and I invested it. I wasn't doing drugs at that time, but my estranged wife was still into the drug scene. I became a workaholic because I felt I had to make up for everything. I felt like a cripple.

"I found myself in trouble with the law. People began to tell me that they were afraid of me, but I couldn't hear what they were saying. I felt that my violent demeanor, my sudden death attitude was right; I had earned it. I became unresponsive to friendship. By nineteen seventy-one I was bitter and didn't care about anything or anyone. I didn't like the way I was being treated by the people back home. I couldn't stand the thought of people feeling sorry for me. One day I took a look at my rich ex-wife, my new home and business, and my child whom I never saw, and realized that I couldn't do what they wanted me to do. I couldn't live up to their expectations, and I became severely depressed.

"One day I picked up my gear and drove off to the woods of Alaska and refused to come out. My wife, thinking she was doing the right thing, sent the police after me. In the ensuing battle, they shot me in the face, and the next week they killed the only one good friend I had. It made me angry, and it started a five-year battle. I never fired on them in anger. They chased me for four years, and I finally spent two years in prison for it.

"I was sent to a VA hospital because, while I was in prison, I had a complete nervous breakdown. I was excommunicated by my church, finally divorced by my wife, and disowned by my family. That saved my life. I finally realized that the path I had chosen in life was wrong.

"I was one of the first documented cases of post-traumatic stress disorder. In those days they simply said I snapped under pressure and took the violent way out. When I was released from prison, they thought I was going to go to the VA hospital. I was still angry and I didn't know what I was angry at. I went back to Alaska where I wasn't supposed to go. I wanted to be in the wilds again where no one could bother me. I wanted to find peace in my life. I just walked off into the woods and lived. They caught up with me and threatened to put me back in jail, so I moved to Washington State where I bought a piece of land. I finally went to the VA and told them I needed help. I had developed colon cancer. They had no records of me. I got angry then because I had fought for two years in Vietnam and now they said I didn't even exist. It took me seven years and five appeals, but finally, in nineteen eighty-three, I won PTSD compensation to go along with my physical disability. I couldn't work. No one wanted a one-armed man.

"I write now. I write stories and put them in a box. It's good therapy for me. I began to reach out and help other Vietnam veterans. I've been to Point Man Ministries many times, and it's helped me. I have a route I make every month. Out of the four or five hundred vets that live in this area, I probably know half of them. I'm welcome in their homes. I've walked into the middle of attempted suicides, I've delivered their babies, fed them when they're hungry and, most of all, I've never told them they were wrong.

"I never thought that I could make a difference until I did. I went out there and did the best I could do, and it made a difference. I'm not bitter about the war. It was just a war, something that happened. It was a job, something that we had to do.

Sgt. Jake

"You can't go out here and kill a man's brother, his daughter, or his children and then expect him to sign a piece of paper and say it's over. You can't get peace by fighting a war. You can't say everything is back to normal because it's not. That bitterness is something that has to die with that generation. When you take a handful of young guys out here and turn them into screaming military fanatics, teach them to kill, you can't bring them home unbriefed, untrained, and expect them to be normal. The first thing you have to teach them to be good soldiers is that they are not normal; they are not average. They are absolutely the best; they are going to win. Nobody ever won a fight thinking he was going to lose."

Dan

U.S. Army

"I entered the U.S. Army in nineteen sixty-seven at the age of seventeen. I went through basic training at Fort Benning, Georgia. They sent me to Airborne school there, and eventually I got my orders to Vietnam. I arrived in the Republic of Vietnam in June of nineteen sixty-eight. I was a little naïve about where I was going. It was quite a sight for me. Flying into the country, I noticed a lot of smoke, and I started getting apprehensive.

"After we landed, and I got off the aircraft; I started noticing the smells and the different looks of people. The country to me had a real smell of death. That's the only way I could possibly describe it.

"I kept hearing explosions and saw the wounded coming in to the hospital there. I saw a lot of wounded just in my three days at Long Binh Airbase. At night the explosions would get louder, and in the daytime they would subside a little. I was given orders to a company of second field forces which I can't disclose at this time because my records are listed as sensitive.

"My stay was quite interesting. I felt all alone when I first arrived there, with everyone staring at me and checking me out. Now I know it was because I was a new guy, and it was a normal thing to do. I was told that I had a relatively safe duty. It made me feel a little bit more comfortable. My first night on guard duty was interesting, and I remember it well. The guy in the bunker with me described my duties. Then he started to tell me about the Tet offensive in nineteen sixty-eight. It was expected to return the next January. He told me everything I had to look forward to. That night I woke up and heard a buzzing noise. I asked what it was, and he said it was 'Puff the Magic Dragon.' I asked him what that meant. All I could see was red coming from out of the sky. He told me it was our AC-47 gunship.

"The longer I was there the more nervous I became. I started to drink more and more. It turned out to be the only way I could unwind and forget that people were coming and going and dying. We'd sit on bunkers at night and hear recordings on the radio. They would tell us we were fighting a losing battle, and that we should come over to their side. It seemed like they were trying to harass us.

"There'd be times when there was nothing going on, but sooner or later they would come back. I felt very inadequate. A lot of times we were ordered not to fire, and eventually it became an irritation to me and the others in the unit. We started to wage our own war. There were real tragedies that happened that still haunt me today.

"Soon I was drinking two fifths of whiskey at a time when I could get it. I spent six months in Vietnam drunk, but I didn't ever use any of the drugs. I didn't realize at that time that alcohol was a drug, too.

"I got slightly injured in one attack and was down for about three weeks. I eventually came home and landed at Travis Air Force Base. There I had my first introduction to the war protesters. I thought I had just left the enemy.

"I had orders to go to Alabama, but I went to Texas instead. I stayed there for awhile and then went to Arizona. They finally caught up with me and sent me back to Alabama. I was reduced in rank, but it didn't bother me. I was still drinking whiskey. The Army decided to put me on medication, and still I drank.

"Eventually I was court-martialed over disrespect to an officer. I went AWOL for a year. I met my future wife during that year. She was the reason that I turned myself back in to straighten my life out. That marriage didn't work. I was having flashbacks, and I did all kinds of crazy things.

"I met Judy at a bar one day. She was singing, and I eventually married her. We moved to the woods, seven miles from the nearest phone, because I wanted to be alone. I didn't need anyone else but her. I was in total isolation from civilization. I was still drunk all the time, and Vietnam was always on my mind.

"One day I was in the woods, and a couple of explosions went off near me. I hadn't been expecting them, and the next day I woke up in jail. I didn't know why I was there. The explosions had apparently set me off in a flashback. I made it home, and I lost complete control. I almost killed my family which I still have a hard time accepting. I started getting help there. The justice system wanted to prosecute me. Some veterans became interested in my case because they recognized that I was suffering from PTSD. I had thought I was back in the jungle of Vietnam when I almost killed my wife and children. I was eventually sent to a mental hospital in Washington.

"They found I suffered from chronic post-traumatic stress disorder from my time in Vietnam. This was the first time I had been aware of this disorder. Since then I've been learning. I still have the nightmares and flashbacks, but at least I can now understand why. I now have a desire to help other veterans who suffer from this disorder. The only way to do this is to listen when they need to talk.

"I've been hospitalized five times and been through the PTSD program. I've been diagnosed as having PTSD, but the Veterans Administration doesn't want to compensate me. I don't get any disability for my sickness, even though it's totally ruined my adult life at this point. I've been marked criminally insane by the justice system, been ridiculed on television and in the news media, and to this day the compensation for this has been nonexistent. It's been a struggle.

"I have three children. Sometimes when they come home from school, they tell me that other children are asking if their father is still crazy. I was forced to sell my home, and I'm planning to move from this area for the welfare of my children. It is not their fault. There is a lack of education about this disorder. They just don't know.

"There were a lot of things missing from my life, and one of those was spirituality. That's something I really had to research and reach out and grab. That's the only thing that's gotten me where I am and is keeping me there. I have hope. I'm not going to let people keep me in the mud. I know there's hope, and I've seen people get through it.

"The effects of PTSD affected my family. My wife told me that while I was away, my son would wake up screaming in the middle of the night. He told her he was dreaming about the war, the Vietnam War. He was nine years old, and he started to isolate himself. He had a lot of anger. It brings a lot of guilt on my part that he had to suffer along with me.

"My wife is the best thing in my life. She has been strong through it all. She's been through as much as I have. I would say that the twenty years I've been home have been exhausting, painful and many times overwhelming to the point of suicide. There have been many times when I've held a gun to my head. It's been a rough road, but I see that there's some light at the end of the tunnel.

"I think the flashbacks and nightmares will always be there, and I think a lot of the sadness will be around for a long time. I have a hard time with the government. I see the boat people coming over here, and that's fine. I know how they lived over there. I see our government setting them up with social security benefits, which they never paid into. I see them with cars and in nice apartments. But the government refuses to provide my benefits for serving in Vietnam. I applied for vocational rehabilitation recently through the Veterans Administration. They denied me because I don't have a thirty percent disability. I applied for social security benefits and was denied. I

Dan

haven't been able to work much since Vietnam because of my PTSD. It's hard to feel comfortable in your own country when they treat the enemy better than those of us who went to fight.

"I feel that the veterans who were willing to give up their lives for their country should not be treated this way by their government. We honored our contracts; they are not honoring theirs. I hold no malice for Southeast Asians in our country. I only hold malice toward our government.

"It's hard to look at my son and realize it won't be long till he's at an age to join the military. It's hard to tell him that he should really fight for his country. It's hard to fight for a government who doesn't honor its own contract. I guess my message to this country is that a house divided will not stand."

Fort Steer

John Steer

It was in 1987 that John Steer began building a place called Fort Steer where Vietnam veterans could go and talk about their problems. There are two lodges there. One serves as a day room, equipped with color television, sofas, chairs, and four offices. The other lodge is a combination kitchen/dining area, and also functions as a meeting hall for seminars, etc. Between the two lodges is a deck, complete with a wheelchair ramp. There is also a block-type shower house, a mobile home, a pavilion and four completed cabins (more are planned).

Few people understand what veterans of war have gone through. They can't understand the pain and utter loneliness that only the veteran can feel in trying to deal with the horrible things he has experienced while serving his country.

We are losing thousands of vets each year to suicide. Substance abuse wards are full and there is a need for a place where veterans and their families can go to receive Christian love and counseling, a place where people understand the veterans' pain and suffering, and where they can work together with others who have dealt successfully with similar problems, such as substance abuse, and where they can finally cope with the everpresent pangs of war that still haunt them and their families. Such a place is Fort Steer in Charlotte, Arizona. The telephone number is 501-799-8111.

There is a campground on its grounds where both cabins and tent sites are available. There are 21 hookups, electricity and water, shower house, and dump station. Enjoy the pavilion on the lake and see the North-Vietnamese guard tower, a POW-MIA memorial. They also offer fishing, swimming, paddle-boating, and many other activities. This veterans' and family retreat center offers clean, wholesome fun for the whole family.

One of Fort Steer's ongoing projects is the construction of a 30 foot POW guard tower with concertina wire around it, "decorated" with dog tags bearing the names of over 2,300 POW-MIAs. Each time a veteran, prisoner of war, or one believed to be missing in action is brought home (alive or dead), his tag will be removed from the tower. The tower is being built, not of granite or brass in order to last for years, but of wood and bamboo, so that upon the resolution of the POW-MIA plight, it can be joyously burned to the ground.

John Steer has traveled all over the United States to minister to other vets. He speaks out, trying to inform the public about the plight of the Vietnam veteran. John was awarded two Purple Hearts, the Silver Star, and the Bronze Star.

John was in the United States Army when he was sent to Vietnam in 1967. He would be out in the field for days on end as they moved further north. He noticed that instead of fighting the local VC, they were fighting crack North Vietnamese Regulars. These men were carrying fully equipped automatic weapons, and had been fighting in the jungle for many years.

He was assigned to A Company, 2nd Battalion, 173rd Airborne Infantry. They were the primary fighting force of any combat unit and would search and destroy the enemy. During one outing John opened fire and saw a North Vietnamese Regular fall. Crawling over to where the body had fallen, he was surprised to see long, flowing hair fall out of the cap. He had killed a young girl.

John was told they would be going down a section of the Ho Chi Minh Trail. They had a new lieutenant who wasn't aware that the troops shouldn't march down an open trail. John tried to dissuade the lieutenant, but was ordered on anyway. He didn't like it, but had no choice.

"We were sent right in the middle of an ambush. Many men were being slaughtered, but we kept on going up the hill. The Vietnamese overran us and killed everyone in sight. Some they tortured; some they just shot in the head. Soon the helicopters came and took the remaining men off the hill."

Then came the battle of Hill 875. This hill had already been taken by Marines, and the Vietnamese had taken it back. It was every man for himself as they fought their way up the hill. John was wounded as he tried to cover for another man. The gooks were coming behind them, in front of them and were everywhere. They didn't know it then, but they were fighting three regiments of North Vietnamese Regulars. They were outnumbered many times over.

He saw arms, legs, heads and bodies lying all around, and John knew they didn't have a chance. He could hear the screams of pain from the dying and could feel blood running down his throat. There was an explosion, and John was thrown many feet in the air. When he tried to touch his face, he couldn't feel his hand. Looking down he noticed that his arm was no longer there. His arm had been blown off. His leg was just hanging on, and he could see body parts all around.

Thinking he would die with the rest of the men, John crawled until he came to a pile of bodies. He pulled a couple of the men over him and passed out. For three days he lay in and out of consciousness until he finally heard help coming. He was taken to the hospital where four surgeons operated for five hours to save his life. He spent two and a half months in ICU in Japan before returning to the States. He didn't lose his leg, but had to have his arm replaced by a hook. John was sent to a VA hospital where he was under psychiatric care for four years. He took Valium to deaden the torment he was going through.

During this time he met a girl and was married. John began to suffer from PTSD, having flashbacks and nightmares. He was consumed by guilt and wanted to go back to Vietnam to fight again. He wanted to kill all those gooks. He felt guilty because he had been spared when so many of his friends had died over in the jungles of Vietnam.

John spent five years living on the dark side of life. He was trying to destroy his life in the only way he knew. He wanted to commit suicide but was afraid of going to hell.

Finally John found God. He realized that God knew what he was going through, and he accepted Jesus into his heart. Since that time John has spent his life trying to help other veterans find the peace that he has found.

John is an accomplished speaker, ministering in word and song. He has a new album/cassette tape available called "Circuit Rider." Also available is his book, *Vietnam, Curse or Blessing*.

Dawn Chavez

Wife of Veteran

"It was nineteen seventy-two when Don and I met at a party. I was barely eighteen years old and full of wonder at all the good things life surely held in store for me. Then this handsome, intelligent, creative young Vietnam veteran entered the scene. Don had just been discharged from his second tour of duty in 'Nam and was embracing life with all the exuberance of an adolescent. Nita, my girlfriend, and I spent the entire evening talking to him. Beyond that evening, however, I hadn't given the matter much thought.

"Imagine my surprise when two weeks later I saw this handsome young man on my doorstep. Surprised, thrilled and nervous, I somehow managed to enjoy our first date. From this point on, Don and I began to build our relationship. I soon learned that Don was a gifted artist and had a vast knowledge concerning many topics. What captivated me most, however, was his kind, gentle nature, and his never-ending curiosity about the hidden treasures of life. While we were growing together in our relationship, I did see signs of inconsistancy in Don's behavior and attitude. I excused any problems, however. Perhaps I believed our love would melt away any problems either of us had. Growing up as a regular viewer of "Leave It to Beaver," I thought my American dream would work out similar to Ward and June's.

"I don't remember ever really discussing Don's experiences in Vietnam. Whenever the subject came up, he would answer briefly and back off. I knew very little about the Vietnam War and had no conception of the day-to-day realities one is faced with in a war.

"In November of nineteen seventy-four, Don and I were married. Our first three years bounced by. The problems we had begun with were continuing to grow. The demand for seclusion from friends and family became stronger for Don so much of our time together was isolated. Don's use of drugs and alcohol continued to increase. Mood swings began to occur more frequently.

From Vietnam to Hell

"Don and I were both working full-time, and our finances were in good standing. However, I quickly learned 'good standing' meant 'look out!' As soon as Don saw things were level, he would change jobs or simply quit.

"Somewhere in our relationship, I found my role as a wife had slowly changed to more of a protective, trapped, mother role. It was a role which I was afraid to abandon, but deeply resented. Coming home from work, I never knew what to expect: an intoxicated husband; a husband high on drugs, sitting in the dark with all the curtains drawn or a great husband full of happiness and greetings. One evening as I came into the house and began to put my things away, I had this strange sensation something was not right. As I walked into the living room, I caught a glimpse of something curled up against the wall. It turned out to be my husband. The look in his eyes and the distortion of his features almost sent me through the wall. I was frightened and bewildered and didn't know what to do. I stood there silently. In a few moments he got up and began to laugh as if it all were a joke. However, the presence I felt in that room and what I saw were no joke to me. That scene stayed in my mind for a long, long time.

"Puzzled and amazed, Don and I continued on. I did notice, at that point, that not a day passed when Don did not take tranquilizers. Looking back on my marriage today, I am baffled at my lack of response to our problems, but life is a learning adventure.

"In nineteen seventy-seven, our lives were once again pretty stable. In that summer, we had our first and only child — a beautiful baby girl. We were both so excited. Don had been at the same job for quite some time, and I had quit working toward the end of my pregnancy. Don was working an evening shift and would arrive home around two in the morning. Usually our daughter was just waking up for feeding, which made us both very happy. Don was able to see her and spend extra time with her. Sometimes we would just sit and marvel at this most beautiful creation after she had gone back to sleep. Our hearts were overwhelmed by the sweetness of this little creation of ours.

"A few months afterwards Don was laid off. It was at this point that he seemed to give up any struggle to maintain the American dream. Things began to move downhill quite rapidly. We lived on our savings for several months, but the money was fast dwindling away, and Don's use of alcohol and drugs doubled. I found my attitude becoming very cold and protective of myself and our daughter. Don and I began to have bitter arguments over finances and concerns for our future.

"During this time all of my protective mothering instincts toward my husband began to crumble. After all the years of nurturing and protecting these problems in my husband's character, I suddenly realized that it was

Dawn Chavez

Dawn and Mirisa Chavez

time he grew up and helped me care for this little daughter we had brought into the world. I believe I was so frustrated with our relationship that I just shut off any emotion in that respect and diverted all my attention to our daughter. There was no sexual relationship between us from that point on.

"For Don it was party time: bars, drugs and the people that came with them. One evening, Don came home at three in the morning, and I was asleep on the couch. I was awakened by his call at the front door. As I opened the door, he tumbled into the room. Full of disgust, I helped him up, closed the door, and tried to lead him to a safe position without allowing him to break the few things left in our home that he had not already broken in fits of rage. He sat on the couch, tilting sideways, begging me to forget everything and let the good times roll! All the love and compassion I had left at that moment could not outweigh my anger, discouragement and fear. Needless to say, I refused my husband's offer. A bang on the the window and a shout beckoning my husband to come on and party some more interrupted our conversation. In spite of my anger, I pleaded with Don to stay home, but he had to go even though he was barely able to walk.

From Vietnam to Hell

"He gathered something from the bedroom, gave me the license plate number to the car and insisted on a kiss goodbye. My pleading made absolutely no difference, and I closed the door with worry, anger and tears.

"The next morning I kept an ear out for his knock and an eye on the window, but it wasn't until early afternoon the knock came at the door. It was not my husband, but a police officer bringing me word that my husband was no longer alive and had apparently created the circumstances himself. In a matter of moments, my life was spinning and crumbling around me. As time passed my life was falling apart. Between guilt and fear of the unknown, I was quickly sinking into a life of despair, self-pity and hardness of heart. My husband's death for me was like a child being left alone in a huge shopping mall, not knowing which direction to turn to for help and transfixed by fear.

"Life was moving all about me, and there I stood dying inside — my American dream stripped away. My little daughter at home counted on me to show her the way, but I had nothing left. I was on empty — physically, mentally, emotionally and spiritually.

"I ended up in the hospital recovering from nervous exhaustion. While recovering in the hospital, my uncle and aunt began to reach out to me. After leaving the hospital, they encouraged me to come and live near them. My grandfather had a lake home neaby, so I rented it. The peaceful surroundings at the lake helped to restore me, but there was still this terrible emptiness within me. My uncle began sharing with me that Jesus Christ was the answer to all my needs. I thought, 'Oh yeah, I've tried that before,' but as time passed, I found loving refuge under the wing of my uncle and aunt. I began to see that their relationship with Jesus and His people really did make a difference in their lives. About six months later, I yielded my life to the Lord.

"Little did I know what the next ten years were to hold. Oh yes, I have had many ups and downs along the way, but because of the sovereignty and mercy of God and His faithful people, my daughter and I are daily growing and maturing into the reality of Christian life. It is strange how when I yielded my will and direction of life to Jesus Christ, I thought I was giving up so much, and in reality, I had nothing to give and nothing to give up. The Lord stood patiently, waiting for me to knock on the door and ask admittance to His life, His kingdom. From that day of entrance, He has been busily making our lives brand new. The Lord placed me under the guidance of a married couple, Mr. and Mrs. Jones. For several years when I would seek guidance and counsel from this couple, I dealt mainly with Mr. Jones. The Lord has used this man to help me mature, like a father with a child. He has also helped heal and restore my respect and trust of men.

Dawn Chavez

"For the past ten years, the Lord has been restoring many areas of my life, and we have touched on but never really examined the area of my marriage. I had pretty much decided to keep going on with the Lord and leave that whole area behind, trusting the Lord to see me through and deal with my life in that area whenever and however He pleased.

"I wished we'd never looked back. But God is in *total* restoration. He is too loving, faithful, and kind to overlook a surrendered cry, a seemingly hopeless cry or perhaps an unconscious cry. He is indeed Lord of all and holds all things together.

"A few months ago Mr. Dean and Mr. Ellis from Point Man Ministries came to our fellowship to share the work the Lord is doing through the ministry. Mr. Ellis captured my attention as he was sharing the characteristics that are commonly found among Vietnam vets. But for me, he was answering many of the unexplained behaviors and attitudes that lived within my husband. I found myself standing and weeping, experiencing a release within me. My husband's dreams had been shattered by death, fear, disillusionment in authority and a fear of the person that now resided within him — this man that could kill and no longer feel. My husband suffered severely from post-traumatic stress disorder. I realized now that PTSD literally enveloped my husband, and the effects tried to invade and envelop my life and my daughter's.

"My daughter and I are now on the road toward recovery, with our heads up, mouths full of pride and hearts resting in His truth, that in all things God works for the good of those who love Him, who have been called according to His purpose. Now when I reflect on my vet, my heart fills with good memories, not anger and regret."

David Knight
U.S. Army

"I went to Vietnam in nineteen sixty-seven as a chaplain in the United States Army. I was with the Mobile Riverine water-born unit. We would look for the VC on search and destroy missions. Our job was to kill or capture the enemy. Because of this, I went in with the men while on these missions. I subsequently ran the same risks as they did and went through the same trauma. I was there when someone was killed or wounded and was able to witness to the love of the Lord. I was also able to assist the medics.

"I got close to a lot of men who were killed or terribly maimed. One of the men that I became close to was named John. We really hit it off, and I would go on many missions with his company. He had only been with us for two weeks when he was killed, and it was a tremendous shock to me.

"I was also close to a sergeant who used to sing "Amazing Grace" at our services. He had a beautiful voice and was a fine Christian who was killed on an operation. He was mistakenly killed by his own men. Still another one I got close to was Tim. We went on 'R and R' together with our wives for two weeks in Hawaii. We had dinner and spent the whole time together. Within two weeks after returning to Vietnam, Tim was wounded when he stepped on a booby trap. I thought his wounds were superficial, but when I came to see him the next morning, learned he had died. This was another very great loss to myself and my wife. In Vietnam, the most important rule was not to get close to anyone because they might get killed, and it would be too painful.

"Although I was a Christian, I still had difficulties sorting this out and went through a lot of trauma saying goodbye to all those boys, knowing I'd never see them again. Consequently I had trouble showing emotion after the war. I never really had the time to work out the emotion of losing these men; however, through the work of the Lord and Point Man Ministries, I've been set free from this emotional trauma.

"I can see that God was able to heal me in this area. Now I can minister

70

to other people who have gone through similar experiences. I've been able to pray with them and counsel with them. One of the things that I think has been beneficial to men who suffer the trauma has been to go back to Vietnam. Recently with these men, I went back to Vietnam, to the places where they fought their battles and went through all sorts of harrowing experiences. It's helped them to realize that the war was not the end, but could be the beginning of a new life in Christ. I've been working with wives and children who have been hurt by the war and done some counseling in that area as well. I kept a diary of the days when we were in Vietnam and will share that with you now."

January 9, Bangkok, Thailand: "The Air France 747 to Vietnam was delayed and gave us ten Christian vets representing 'Vets with a Mission' time to build relationships with one another. It also gave us time to see the 500 Bibles in Vietnamese that we will be taking with us to Vietnam. This shipment, hopefully, will be the first consignment of 5,000 such Bibles to be shipped while we are there. The Bibles were given by Vietnamese pastors in the States and have been stored in Bangkok until we are ready to enter SRV."

January 10, SRV Ho Chi Minh City: "We spent the first night in Vietnam in an old war-time hotel, the Caravelle, which has been renamed the Hoc Lap by the new regime. It was in the lobby of this very hotel in 1968 that the VC placed a bomb which subsequently exploded and killed numerous American servicemen.

"Coming back after 21 years was a somewhat emotional experience. It brought to mind some things that we didn't want to remember. However, because God is with us, He has dispelled the oppression.

"Today we went to the polio orphanage in HCM City, a place assigned to us for humanitarian aid. We were shocked to see 250 crippled children on crutches and in braces. It was a scene reminiscent of the thirties and forties in the USA before the advent of polio vaccine. Evidently, this present regime has the vaccine but is unable to effectively vaccinate children in the rural areas. Either they don't have the personnel to do so, or the people are reticent about instituting such a program.

"Our bus driver for this trip is a former North Vietnamese Army veteran who used to drive a truck on the Ho Chi Minh Trail. He was quite open about this, also very friendly with us, his former foes. This seems to be the attitude of many of the VC and NVA veterans we have met so far. Tonight, Roland, the Bolsa Tour leader who set up this trip for us, took us to Maximes, an old French restaurant. It was a popular place for the Russians and the Vietnamese.

"Again we encountered a former NVA soldier, a friend of Roland's, who

71

From Vietnam to Hell

David Knight

also was in a very conciliatory mood. He fought at Khe San and described how afraid he was of going into battle against the Marines. He said he was so afraid that when he was alone he would cry. Jack Ernest, one of our vets and a former Marine at Khe San, said he had the same nightmares about battles with the NVA.

"These miraculous circumstances have caused us to believe that a sit-down dinner with some of our former foes might be a real opportunity to witness to the forgiveness of the Lord and the possibility of being reconciled."

January 11: "Arrived at the Da Nang Airport from HCM City aboard an old and somewhat decrepit TU 134 Russian jet. At the airport we met CBS reporter, Pattie, who works with Morley Safer on the '60 Minutes' segment dealing with NVA and VC veterans and wants to include us, their former foes, in the story. We were subsequently videotaped in Da Nang by Pattie who likes the idea of a sit down dinner with our former foes. We

David Knight

then travelled to China Beach where we are to stay for several days as guests of the office of Vietnam tourism. China Beach is a beautiful place. It looks a lot like pictures of Bali. During the war there was a large US hospital here, and it is the place depicted in the TV series 'China Beach,' on CBS which describes the trials and tribulations of the US nurses during the war."

January 13: "Left China Beach this morning for Hue, the old Royal capital of Vietnam and an area where there was terrible fighting during the Tet offensive. It was raining when we left, and the rain increased as we crossed Hayvan Pass on Highway I. This area brought back a lot of memories for some. We passed places like Red Beach and Phu Bai where battles were fought with the VC and NVA near Highway I, the main artery running north and south. Roger Helle, for example, showed us where he was wounded and his squad ambushed. I'm sure this drive conjured up all sorts of feelings for him and many others.

"We arrived in Hue about noon and settled into our new home, the Huong Giang Hotel. I got a nice room by Vietnamese standards on the second floor where we could look across the Song Huong River at the Imperial City. The city itself is reminiscent of the pictures of the forbidden city in the recent film, 'The Last Emperor.' The last king of Vietnam, the Boa Daj, is still alive. He is 82 and lives in Paris, France. He left Vietnam and the Imperial City in 1945."

January 15: "After breakfast we left Hue for a tour of Ho Chi Minh Trail and Khe San. The highway is rough and bumpy. Indeed, some of the bridges looked none too safe. However, after 100 miles of being jostled and jerked around, we arrived at the beginning of the infamous Ho Chi Minh Trial, which is now a paved road of some 5,000 miles. It starts in Hanoi and twists its way through Laos and Cambodia into Vietnam. We didn't travel the entire 5,000 miles, but we did go far enough to realize the effort and the commitment it must have taken to build it and rebuild it after the Americans had bombed it. The country it travels through is very beautiful. It is much like the North Cascades Highway in Washington State without the snow.

"After we left the Ho Chi Minh Trail, we travelled to Khe San, a place well remembered by many of the vets as a place where 6,000 Marines kept 30,000 NVA at bay for 56 days during some of the heaviest fighting of the war.

"We had some difficulty finding the place, but finally with the help of some of the local Vietnamese we found it. It was an awesome and somewhat fearsome experience to see this battlefield littered with debris from 12 years ago. There were unexploded rounds and a windswept silence that

73

gave it an eerie feeling. We left Khe San in shocked silence at what we had seen and experienced."

January 16, Hue: "At 9:00 a.m. we left for Da Nang and our return flight to Ho Chi Minh City and the last leg of our journey."

January 17: "Left on an early flight from Da Nang to Ho Chi Minh City. Traveled with the international set that has been so much a part of our journey. There were Russians, East Germans, French newspaper people, American journalists, etc. Several American media people, including Joan Epezito from Channel 7 in Chicago, who had interviewed us the night before, were on board. Everyone seemed happy to be leaving for the sunny South except maybe the Russians who always seemed somber.

"We arrived in mid-afternoon at Tan Son Nhut airport in HCM City and once again settled into the Caravelle Hotel. We ate across the street at the Rex Hotel which is the only place in HCM City where you can get western food. I have enjoyed Vietnamese food, but am getting a little weary of it."

January 18, HCM City: "Awakened to a beautiful sunlit day in old Saigon. Today we are scheduled to visit Mr. Nguyen Van Chi, director of the Social Welfare Department in Ho Chi Minh City, and then visit the polio orphanage, our first major humanitarian project in SRV.

"Our visit to Mr. Chi and his assistant, Mr. Niehm, was pleasant but businesslike. As we drank tea, we discussed our involvement at the polio orphanage and what they would expect us to do. As of now, we have pledged $8,000 to restore the wading pool, the bathrooms, the playground, etc.

"Indeed, our next visit will involve vets with building skills starting all of these projects.

"Our next stop was the orphanage where we were joyfully received by Sister Elizabeth, the staff and the children.

"These children are really a sight to behold. They have every reason to be unhappy. They have been crippled by poliomyelitis and have to wear braces and use crutches the rest of their lives.

"They also have been deserted by their families, the ultimate rejection. Yet I never saw a happier group of children. Truly the love of God manifested itself in them.

"In order to respond to their love, we used this as an opportunity to give them the many presents we had brought from the States. This included the package of things Pat had put together for this occasion before I left, plus the Vietnamese money I had held back for this moment. It also included some personal gifts of US currency by some of the men. One man, for example, gave $500 in US currency, a tremendously valuable gift in Vietnam.

74

"I then had the distinct pleasure of praying on this occasion and immediately felt the power of the Holy Spirit rise up in all of us as I asked for the reconciliation of the American and Vietnamese people and God's blessing upon this occasion. Sister Elizabeth, who normally is quite restrained, was visibly affected and Hinh, our guide from Hanoi, was unabashedly affected and began to cry. Again the Holy Spirit was present to release His love and joy."

January 19, HCM City: "We learned last night that the 4,500 Bibles may not be shipped on Air France. Evidently there is a problem either with the goverment or with Air France or both.

"Undoubtedly the enemy is the real culprit. Upon hearing this news we began to pray that the Bibles would be shipped and that the enemy would be bound. We met in groups of two or three and brought our concerns before Him, 'the giver of all good gifts.'"

January 20, HCM City: "The Bibles still have not arrived. Nor has Roland, our tour director, and our last hope for getting the Bibles into HCM City. Again we prayed before the throne of grace.

"Tonight we had a sit-down dinner with our former enemies, the NVA and the VC at the home of the NVA major who had fought the Marines at Khe San. In attendance also were Morley Safer and his camera crew, including Pattie, from CBS. It was both a tense event and an exciting one. Before the meeting we prayed that any animosities we felt toward our former foes would be removed by the Holy Spirit and that we would be able to love our enemies and manifest Christian love. I believe our prayers were answered, for we showed genuine love and forgiveness. I don't know how '60 Minutes' will portray this, but I believe that it was a real victory for the Lord. I can only hope that God can use it as a step toward reconciliation."

January 21: "Today was a glorious day in HCM City. We had just found out that our prayers had been answered, and the Bibles are here, praise God! We don't know how or when they came, but when Bill Kimball and Hinh went to the airport, they were there — all 4,500 of them. Truly our God is a great God! Today we were also interviewed on video by a Hollywood film producer who is doing a documentary on vets returning to society. It will be called, 'Going Home.' Our hearts weren't really in this, but were with those Bibles and the people that will receive them tomorrow at the Tin Lanh Church, the Evangelical Church of Vietnam."

January 22, HCM City: "We left for the church via rickshaws and arrived in time to greet the pastors and the people before the service. I felt a real spiritual bonding with the pastors who were there to greet us. They represented some thirty-seven churches in HCM City and five hundred churches in all of Vietnam. They were overjoyed to see us and told us how happy they were to receive these 5,000 Bibles for the people of Vietnam. They also said that they hoped we would have a long and profitable relationship.

"For me and the other vets, it was a very significant and spiritually moving time. These are the saints that kept the fires of Christianity alive through some very difficult and trying years. All of them had been in prison or re-education camps because of their faith, and one, the senior pastor, had spent over fifteen years in prison. As John the Revelator puts it, 'These are those who have come out of the Great Tribulation.' And these are those who should give the Word of God to the people.

"On January 22, we returned to the States. We had come to Vietnam in faith believing that God wanted us there and praying that He would protect and guide us; we were not disappointed. For indeed, He did protect us, and he was a Lamp unto our Feet. If we had been able to do nothing more than bring in 5,000 Bibles, it would have been enough, but because God is God, He did much more."

Fred Love

U.S. Marines

"I trained in Special Operations for thirteen months prior to reporting to Danang, Vietnam. I arrived late in the afternoon, and our group was immediately mortared by twenty enemy rounds. I was ordered to Hill 37 and assigned to 3rd Battalion, 7th Marines. Battalion assigned me to 'Suicide India.' This would be my 'mother' unit for the next fourteen months.

"There are many covert teams operating in S.E. Asia, but very few specially trained Marine Special Operations Teams. We (Marines) had our own special forces known as Force Recon, and their job was to secure information on enemy activities and report this back to Battalion. We received certain assignments which took us outside the national boundaries of South Vietnam on many occasions.

"I would receive messages from Danang. If written or verbal orders called for the elimination of a double agent village chief, then I would draw up plans for his hasty demise. It became impossible to remove him without injuring innocent parties, so an incident was created which removed everyone in his group. Yes, this was cold-blooded, but war tends to transform the man on the street into a well trained-killing machine.

"The night was warm with a gentle breeze coursing through the broad leaves and twisted mass of broken twigs. My point had been instructed to approach a quiet little French villa located in Antenna Valley, five clicks from hill ten. About halfway down, I held up the patrol to get a last good look of the area we were to enter. We remained in place for ten minutes, looking for any movement in the forward areas.

"Everything appeared normal, and I motioned the point to begin his approach to the villa. We walked through the brush, turning left, then right, as the patrol moved quietly through the hilly terrain. The patrol moved closer to the small wall surrounding the villa with no incidence. As we came within a few feet of the pale white-washed wall, I had everyone get down and crawl to the small defensive.

From Vietnam to Hell

"Just as the point rose to his feet, automatic rifle broke the still silence. Rounds tore up the earth in front of us, throwing clumps of dirt and debris into our faces. 'Grenade!' I yelled. It detonated somewhere between the wall and building. The Marines gave cover fire as two men and I ran for a small structure ten meters away. We opened fire on the house as we ran full tilt for cover. Bullets spit fire as they ricocheted in all directions upon striking the concrete wall.

"I was within a few meters of the open doorway when the barrel of an AK protruded through the window. The AK struck my flack jacket in the right breast area and spun me around a half turn, and I fell face down in the trampled sod. Firing was all around me as I gathered my wits, got to my feet and assaulted the front door. I raked the room with semi-automatic fire.

"I saw five NVAs on the concrete floor obviously blown to hell. Pieces of flesh, bone and bloody clothing were scattered around the room like trash. Large pools of blood spilled out across the dirty floor as scarlet splashes trickled down the walls. Death's eyes stared at me as my face flinched from nervous tension — the moment stolen from a scene of the 'Twilight Zone.'

"Suddenly, pockets of enemy troops opened on us from virtually every corner of the perimeter. I crawled to the shed where the squad was held up. I tried to yell over the noise that we were in one hell of a situation. I told them to move it, to run across the clearing. Rounds cracked around us as every Marine ran into the front room. Our best plan of defense would be to make position inside the house and avoid a disaster. We'd been surrounded long before entering this villa. If they successfully overwhelmed us, any survivors could be captured and whisked to the Ho Chi Minh Trail a few hundred meters away. The survivors would be in Hanoi by the week's end if they weren't killed on the march.

"Meanwhile India advised they were dispatching reactionary to help us as rounds changed to high explosives. The house next to us was leveled by a single 155 round. Both doorway and wall began to crumble as I yelled cease fire. Our reactionary had come under heavy fire about halfway to us, so I began to nervously finger the single .223 round that I kept in the pen pocket of my flack jacket. It had been placed there months earlier in preparation for what I was now facing. It would be my way out if the gooks took us prisoners. I refused to be taken alive, especially after I had seen what they do to prisoners.

"Less than a minute later, the NVA launched a frontal assault on our shattered fortress. 'Fix bayonets,' I yelled. Everyone that wasn't firing removed their long knives and strapped them into our weapons. As bayonets were fixed, a small fire flared near the radio. I put my right hand on Doc's shoulder and said, 'This is it, Doc. God be with us.'

"Everything seemed to be blowing up before our very eyes as the artillery fell on our little home away from home. The very building we were in began to collapse as two rounds hit with devastating effect. Everyone was scared to death as shells tore at the building and airburst shook us to our marrow. Several assault troops made it to the door against the intense fire power and rushed through the collapsed opening. Sounds of metal against metal, people yelling and screaming in two languages combined with rifle fire and bursting artillery rounds melted together in horror.

"I heard a voice in Vietnamese not far from me in the blackness and without hesitation thrust my rifle forward. The blade struck the man, entering his torso to the hilt, as I screamed in anger. I began twisting the flimsy weapon in an effort to dislodge the bayonet. As I gritted my teeth, nearly breaking their caps, the NVA yelled with a gurgling sound. It changed into a grunting sound as the impaled soldier turned and twisted to dislodge my instrument of death. 'Get off! Get off!' I yelled frantically. 'Get off my damned rifle you miserable bastard!' He fell limp as I finally used the only idea I had to remove the bayonet. I fired as I jerked back on the pistol grip and forearm. This freed my weapon. His body fell limp in a heap on the floor as I stumbled over another one behind me. I had no more than hit the floor when someone's boot stomped my right forearm, nearly fracturing the bones. All around me I heard men groaning, begging for help, calling for their mothers and mamasans. It was pure hell.

"Suddenly I began to laugh. In the midst of all the death and confusion I simply laughed aloud for no reason. As I assumed an upright position, someone hit me in the stomach with a rifle or elbow. I fell to the floor vomiting. With vomit all over me, I tried to get my breath when I was struck on the side of the head with an unseen object. The blow left me spinning on the floor, and I blacked out. When I came around, my mouth was full of dirt from the cement floor. The battle raged on, so I knew I hadn't been out for more than a half minute as I staggered to my feet. There was no leadership, no control at all. Everyone was his own commander as we fought in the blackness of this ancient French villa. I no longer thought of the doc, my team or the reactionary. My only thoughts were those of total survival.

"Working my way to the collapsed doorway, I shoved my M-16 through the debris and fired at several figures running across the front yard. After wounding three or four, I pulled back and grabbed the handset again. This time I began to yell, 'Fire mission, fire mission, fire mission.'

"India responded. I requested fire immediately. 'We have an overrun situation,' I yelled. India acknowledged my request, and seconds later the earth began to move as the shattering reports of artillery began to fall. The forces outside had taken cover as artillery burst over them, but a new, more welcomed sound met my ears through the barrage. I heard the sound of approaching choppers. Their mini-guns were bringing devastation in the distance, and a few reporting rockets were fired on the enemy.

"No one was left but me, so I decided to destroy everything. We would simply be some yellowed page in a dusty history book one hundred years from now.

"While I surveyed the devastated room, I saw two tanks rumble by. One moved directly across the span yard with guns lowered. The tank slid to a stop with its barrel nearly touching the earth as another one pulled along side of it. The first one began rotating on one track and aimed its big gun toward our little fortress. 'Here it comes,' I thought to myself.

"With barrel positioned, someone on the machine yelled, 'Hey, any jarheads in there?' I yelled for them to hold their fire and walked through the debris to the tanks. One of the soldiers brought out a Vietnamese soldier with my K-bar sticking from his chest. His head had been turned completely around. It was sickening.

"As the sun rose over the distant ridge, the welcome light shone on a most hellish sight. The hamlet was nothing more than rubble as I wandered out towards the gate for an overall view. The large trees I had fear of earlier were splintered by artillery and mini-guns. The buildings and small sheds could not have been dealt a deadlier blow by a wrecking crew, as timbers protruded from the fallen roof and crumbled walls like fingers of death poised for their next victim. The grounds surrounding the concrete structures were pockmarked with the previous night's artillery strike and rocket attacks from both friend and foe.

"While looking over the devastation, I placed my battered M-16 in one hand and began turning in circles. Around and around and around I turned — spinning the death away from me. The world wasn't the same in my dizzy state of mind. I spun until my equilibrium failed, throwing me to the ground with a thud. I lay there for several moments as everything remained distorted and out of focus. 'Will this ever end?' I thought. 'Will this nightmare never end?'

"My group had been on an extended campaign to search out and destroy the enemy. By this point in my tour, I had become a point man and due to my smaller size, had been trained as a 'tunnel rat.' The operation had been very bloody for both friend and foe. Of the original one hundred ninety Marines that had entered the field of battle, only forty-seven were left to fight. I had moved from point man through 2nd fire team leader, finally to squad leader in less than three weeks.

"I had caught shrapnel in both legs and in my right ankle. We had been in monsoon rains for fifteen straight days. My feet had developed infections called cellulitus, emersion foot, and jungle rot from the imbedded shrapnel. You can imagine the unbearable pain.

"Both pus and blood oozed from the dried holes in my jungle boots, and to make matters worse, my woolen socks had grown to the flesh on my feet. We had no clean socks in the battlefields, and I asked the corpsman about Medivac and he tagged me. The platoon leader said they couldn't spare me so I remained in the field another full day and was in such pain that I stood when engaging the enemy just to get shot to leave the bush.

"A battle ensued shortly afterwards, and we fought through a graveyard where my squad found a tunnel. I threw a gas canister in and, putting on my gas mask, entered the tunnel. A rifle butt hit me in the right knee, and I grabbed the weapon and slid it back behind me. I escorted the two NVA out as prisoners of war. I moved back and was asked to take the prisoners back when I was Medivaced. I agreed, and the three of us sat down on a rice paddy dike. I had three Winston cigarettes which I shared. Their war was over, I thought. The two enemy soldiers were about fifteen to seventeen years old, and they were pleased with my kind jesture and smiled. Three warriors sitting there in the middle of the battlefield enjoying a cigarette.

"We boarded the chopper and were taken away. Throughout the lengthy flight, the gunner would reach over and hit first one, then the other prisoner. I didn't like this, but I was on someone else's turf so I said nothing. Upon arriving, the NVA were the first two out, courtesy of the gunner. He simply threw them out some fifteen feet above the ground. I really didn't like this. It did nothing to improve relations with those villagers that watched in pure fear. Word came to me later that both NVA succumbed to cardiac arrest during interrogation, which is completely illogical to say the least. I could have gotten more valuable information from these two, had I not been on my way to the hospital.

"Sometimes when I reflect back to my 'glory days' of Marine Corps service, I wonder if it was worth it. Were my duties in Southeast Asia really worth the pain and mental anguish? My mother once told me, 'The Fred I knew died in Vietnam,' and that statement has bothered me for many, many years.

"I crushed a wrist in Vietnam and was brought to the hospital. The arm was so badly swollen that the first cast applied had to be removed seven days later. Once the second cast was removed the arm showed an obvious deformity. I continued to experience pain and discomfort for the remainder of my tour, but nothing was done to correct the problem. The goverment was keeping me hidden away in the jungle and appeared to be denying my injury as serious enough for consideration.

"After returning to Stateside at Camp Lejeune, I was placed on all sorts of duties. It was during this time that they had what was called an 'early out program.' It was only for those who had served a full term in Vietnam. As much as my unit hated to do it, they offered the release program to me in place of another fulltime duty in Vietnam. They offered me a promotion and cash bonus to return, but there was no way I would go back to leading patrols into those fearful gray-blue mountains in Vietnam. Just the thought of a helicopter assault brought flooding memories of the helicopter crash in nineteen sixty-eight that nearly drowned me in a rice paddy.

"I accepted the honorable discharge and left the Marine Corps. The next twenty years I would attempt to get my arm attended to at various VA hospitals, and for all that time I was told there was nothing wrong with my arm. Senator San Nunn had St. Louis Records Center send me a copy of my medical and military SRB.

"The Disabled American Veterans served as my representatives and, when I was given an appointment for re-evaluation, I took my medical records. The VA doctors were surprised when I submitted my records as evidence to the injury. I was finally awarded disability compensation. Many Vietnam veterans received similar treatment until just a few years ago, when news hit the airwaves about the Veterans' Administration's callous approach to veterans. It caused the VA to take a closer look at the war veteran's, and I feel sure many eventually received compensation for injuries received on the battlefield.

"Nearly everyone that served in combat saw the Puff ship in action on more than one occasion. Every time a major offensive at night was underway, Puff gave air support. Each time my unit was overrun, Puff was there with its three mini-guns blazing. One of these crafts was shot down in the mountains, and my unit had to go in and retrieve the seven crewmen and any equipment left intact. We found it burned to a crisp and only skeletal remains of the seven-member crew. They were carried out of the jungle in one poncho. This was very saddening and demoralizing for my group, for we had received help from these men on several occasions and now they were no more. It was like losing seven good friends even though we had never met them personally.

"There are over one hundred thousand Vietnam veterans in prisons, an additional two hundred thousand are on parole, between twenty-six thousand and one hundred thousand have committed suicide since returning from the killing fields, and an additional fourteen thousand (estimate) commit suicide annually (usually single car accidents).

"Vietnam held me down for years. I had reported to Vietnam with a joyful spirit and a desire to liberate those people from the communists. Three months into the tour had changed these into thoughts of self-preservation and total survival.

"On October the ninth, I had paid a final visit to my company in the bush and bid them farewell. It was a saddening event, of which I have relived the moment on many occasions. As I write, I can see their faces still coming through the mists of time. No one was happy that solemn rainy day. The men felt I was their lucky charm. 'No one had survived this long,' one man was heard to say. I had mixed emotions. I felt guilty for leaving these inexperienced men in the bush, and I was joyous for having survived more than a full tour.

"After returning to the world I was placed in charge of small units tactics with the 8th Marines located at Camp Lejeune. I was also made Brig Chaser for this regiment which kept me on call a great deal of my free time. I drank at every chance, but never on duty. Due to a broken love affair, I refused to allow myself to get close to any one woman. My fiancé broke off our engagement while I was in combat, and this made me very distrustful of any close relationships.

"I involved myself in fist fights and drunken sprees at the slightest provocation. I was a very bitter individual. I was honorably discharged in July nineteen sixty-nine.

"Upon reaching my parents' home, I immediately took residence and solitude in my old room. There, I would remain unless at work. My drinking progressively grew worse, and I began to fraternize with married ladies only. In this way I would not become emotionally involved because they belonged to someone else. My anger was released on anyone that challenged me.

At age twenty-nine, I met my present wife and we have two daughters, one age ten and the other fourteen. My wife had been married and divorced before we met. She had one child.

"One day my wife asked me to get rid of some unwanted puppies. She left to visit with her family while I took care of the gruesome details. I loaded my shotgun, drank four beers and walked to my uncle's to collect the 'victims' for transport. While walking through some of the thick brush, a tree limb struck my face. All of a sudden I wasn't in the US, I was in Vietnam again. My M-16 (shotgun) became entangled with some honeysuckle, and I began to wrestle a 'Viet Cong.' I stomped his throat and fired my weapon into my foot (his head). When I awoke, I was face down in the pine straw with my mouth full of dirt. One of the puppies I was to shoot licked my face as I lay there in pain. This had been one of my worst flashbacks, which cost me a toe and its joint. The entire episode was so real that I could smell 'Vietnam.'

"Sometimes I would wake up in a closet, and my wife would tell me that I'd had another nightmare. She was disturbed by my actions and the constant drinking. I began to fabricate weapons from anything and everything. When someone crossed me, I would study them in detail, fabricate extravagant plans for their hasty demise and make practice runs. I once threatened to blow up an entire textile mill which was one mile long. It stands to reason that I was fired from this company.

"Another time I had been drinking and decided to take my yellow jeep for a drive. A patrol car tried to pull me over, and I accelerated it. I headed for the interstate and noticed that more police cars were following me, now with blue lights flashing. As I sped along, I lost track of reality and became disoriented. The law became the VC, and I was a patrol leader engaged in escape and evasion. I hit a ditch and my engine stopped. As I reached to crank it, I felt a .357 Magnum slip under my ear. The owner simply stated, 'I wouldn't do that Fred.' My mind went over the edge. I began giving my name, rank, and serial number. I handed the 'NVA' my military ID card. The officer was immediately surrounded by fifteen deputies. Two officers eased me into the back of the car and said they were sending me to Alabama. I told them to get help for my men as the Viet Cong were everywhere. I was handcuffed and taken to Lanette. They called the VA hospital and asked what to do with me. The VA remained on standby all night with a padded truck and straitjacket. The next morning I was allowed to go home.

"In nineteen eighty-five I was born into Christ, and my flashbacks, nightmares and many other PTSD symptoms dissipated. There are residues of the war that will always be with me, but I was delivered of my daily drinking problem instantly. I haven't had a desire for alcohol since. And I seriously doubt that I shall ever go back that way again.

"I began to counsel 'Nam vets for several months, but it started getting to me and I was forced to bow out. There is simply so much about my tour that can't be discussed, that I felt it unfair to ask others to share what really bothered them.

"Life isn't a bed of roses. There are thorns scattered helter-skelter throughout the paths, highways and by-ways. Sometimes situations bring out a burst of anger, but the difference is this: when I do mess up, I will apologize as opposed to before.

"Even though most of the PTSD has gone, I still have trouble sleeping at night. This has been a problem for me for over twenty years. I am presently enrolled with Liberty Bible College. It's a two year course which is very indepth. I have forty certificates and an additional sixty-four certificates in secular studies. I hold a first degree black belt in karate, kobudo nunchaku. Martial arts is a direct contradiction to scripture, so I gave up the teaching part about the same time I renounced my Master Mason status.

"There are positive approaches to any problems, great or small. The Lord was mine. I had tried everything to help me cope with PTSD, alcohol, drugs, violence, anger, regression, and denial; but Christ is the ONLY answer. There is no middle ground, no neutral territory.

"One can hide in the backwoods alone, and Vietnam can come crashing in at any moment. It's not where one is, but who one is. To feel like a loser is to make oneself a loser. To feel like a winner is to make oneself a winner."

Donna

Wife of Veteran

"'Strength through gentleness,' that's what his name means. That's the type of man I thought I'd married Thanksgiving Day, nineteen eighty. A short six months later, I began to see another side of him that he'd kept hidden from me—that of an angry, troubled man. Much of his past life I've pieced together due to his unwillingness to discuss it with me.

"He came from a strong Italian Catholic background where his mother was very domineering. He had an older sister who was very much like her mother, and his younger brother had severe mental problems. His mind stopped growing from the age of twelve. No one seemed to know why. My husband's early home life was very hard for him, and at the age of fifteen he began to spend more and more time away from home and eventually moved in with another family.

"School was not of much interest to him, and he said even then he felt he didn't fit it. He joined the Army at the age of eighteen and was sent to Vietnam in nineteen sixty-nine with a heavy artillery unit. His job there was to shoot the large gun. The targets were determined by a coordinate passed down from higher command.

"Not knowing who he was shooting at was very hard on him, and he felt the war was a psychological game. He didn't trust anyone. He didn't have any buddies that he talked about, but said he couldn't even trust his bunk buddy. The days and hours spent between battles were difficult for him, too. It gave him too much time to think. With the thinking came memories of guilt, anger and frustration. He became addicted to heroin. He said it helped him to become numb. A little Vietnamese boy was his supplier and his only so-called friend. He spent one and a half years in Vietnam, and before he could go home, he had to go through a detox program to get off the drugs. He was sent home in nineteen seventy-one.

"Upon returning home, he went to see some old friends, one of which was his old girlfriend. In the time he'd been gone she had been dating his

86

Donna

best friend and was no longer interested in him. He was hurt deeply by her rejection and by the loss of his best friend. His family had difficulty with his return.

"He went to live with them, but they didn't know him anymore; he was a different man. He said he felt like a stranger in his own home. He was also upset at the fashion at the time, army fatigues and jackets. It made him very angry because he had earned his fatigues. He felt rejected by everyone who ever knew him and by the country he'd fought for. Feeling very hopeless, rejected and full of despair, he began spending all of his time alone.

"One day while he was at the laundromat, he met a woman who began to speak to him about God. She told how He had set her free and how He could set him free also. As she talked, he told her he'd consider what she had to say. Before going to bed that night he got down on his knees and asked God to show him the truth. As he slept, he dreamed that God came to him and told him how much He loved him and wanted him as His child. The next morning he woke up with a sense of joy and well-being. He wanted to share what he had experienced and started telling his old friends about Jesus. He began attending church. It was held in an old barn, almost like a hippie church. He said it was the first place he felt he could be himself and still be accepted and loved for who he was. Even though God had entered his life, he still carried with him many of the scars and chains of the war. He had severe problems, depression and distrust of authority. He couldn't handle stress and had a tendency toward violence. He'd also learned how to put a wall around his emotions. He began to question God.

"He began to lose his trust in God and began to smoke marijuana to help ease the pain. He decided to leave his home state and family. He decided to make the Pacific his home and began to look for acreage in the mountains of Montana.

"The first stop on his journey was Spokane, Washington. I met him there in the summer of nineteen eighty at a garage sale. He and I talked for several hours, and I found myself falling in love with the most interesting man I'd ever met. He'd been in Spokane about three years by this time, and he had been able to hide many of the stresses. What I saw was a kind and gentle man who loved the Lord. I had accepted the Lord when I was twelve, and it fascinated me to hear him talking about Jesus. We began seeing each other everyday, and on Thanksgiving Day, we were married.

"The first six months of our marriage were wonderful, but as the newness began to wear off, and the pressures of everyday life began to press in, I saw changes in him. Soon our baby son was born, and with him came the reality of responsibility. Our son had some physical problems as a baby

87

From Vietnam to Hell

Donna and her son (October, 1987)

and I'd had some severe problems during labor. This caused my husband to question God and the lives of his new family.

"We eventually purchased some acreage in Idaho and, when my son was two years old, we moved onto the land. We were without water, plumbing and electricity. Our shelter was a box that my husband had built to put on his two-ton truck. We used an old burner to cook on and for heat.

"The days were filled with excitement, getting to know our new land and the neighbors. It was an adventure, and for the first time I saw a smile on my husband's face. But pretty soon winter came, and we had a taste of what it meant to be snowed in. Our property was off the main highway. In order to get to work, my husband would have to park his truck at the foot of the mountain and walk down to it. He would be gone from early morning until late at night. Jobs were hard to find, and sometimes food was pretty scarce.

Donna

"I saw my husband beginning to slip away in a place all his own. He began to push me away even more, ignoring me much of the time. I felt rejected by him and isolated from my family and actually many of my friends because of the way we lived. If it hadn't been for the Lord, I would have lost my mind.

"It did get worse. My husband would pack his rifle and a backpack and, without telling me, would go out in the mountains for several days at a time. He left me alone without any means to get help if necessary. When he was home, he'd tell me to leave.

"I was involved with a church and would go whenever I could. I'd walk to a place where the pastor would pick me up. My husband had stopped attending, and it was through the support of the pastor and my friends that I was able to hang on.

"The most difficult thing for me was to watch my marriage fall apart with something that I was unable to understand or do anything about. This man that I loved so much had become someone I didn't even know. The more I tried to get close, the more he pushed me away. The more he pushed away, the harder I tried to hang on. Finally I felt the only thing I had left to do was to leave as he'd asked me to do a thousand times before. He'd refused to go for counseling, and I was exhausted by his rejection of God's truth, the tearing down of my own self-esteem, and fear for the safety of myself and my son. He had begun to be very violent and was filled with extreme rage which would explode at any time. My son and I moved back to Spokane where we were put in touch with Kings Community Church where we now attend.

"Slowly and painfully we began to put our lives together with the help of some very dear people who laid down their lives for us. I began to learn how much God loved me. I learned too, that I must let God be God, not only in my life, but in my son's life.

"Things seemed to get worse. He committed adultery several times and we finally got a divorce. I was in extreme pain and God picked me up and carried me through.

"About a year ago, two men from Point Man Ministries came to our church to share with us what God was doing through their ministry. I was fascinated by what they had to say about Vietnam vets, and I began to piece the puzzle of my husband's life together. God was answering the questions I had been asking. I began to cry as God's love came around me.

"The last year has been a real triumph. God had brought me through and continues to heal me. It's been an uphill climb, but God has been with me all the way. I know God's not through with me. It's a day to day process. I know God's not through with the man in Idaho — the man who is hiding from reality, from God, and from himself. The man suffers every day, but I know that God can heal him, too.

"I now work for the Homefront Ministries set up for women and children of Vietnam vets and hope to help others who have been where I've been and felt what I've felt."

Larry Hiller

U.S. Marine Corps

"I joined the Marine Corps in nineteen sixty-seven and was sent to Vietnam during some of the fiercest fighting of the war. Most of the time I was point man for my battalion. As point man, you are expected to go ahead of the main group and look for booby traps, land mines, and any other signs of the enemy. The point man makes sure an area is safe for everybody else to come through. I used to pray, even back then, that God would keep us safe so that we could do our duty and get back home safely.

"Vietnam was an extremely hard environment in which to survive. Everything about it was harsh and demanding—the extremes of temperature, the vegetation, the bugs, the snakes. Because of the way the war was being fought it was also very frustrating, and you had a lot of feelings of hopelessness and despair. Consequently, the men that survived Vietnam learned to cope the only way they could, and that was by letting nothing really touch them. You turned off your feelings as part of a defense mechanism so that you could survive.

"I remember sitting and listening to a couple of very foul-mouthed Marines who looked like they'd bite your head off if given a chance. They were coming out of the jungle after serving a year and had lived through hell and were on their way back. I was very conscious of how like animals they were. They were very bitter and ready to strike at any moment.

"Until you actually go over there and step out in the jungle, everything you ever learned was just training for the real thing. We marched up to Khe Sahn to relieve the Army, and I can still smell the stink. It was very warm and heavy and smelled like a damp rag. There were times when the air was so putrid that you had trouble breathing. There were dead bodies all over which added to the smell.

"We tried our hand at some operations. One of the first ones lasted two weeks or more. We chased the Cong, and they would chase us; it went back and forth. I would pray a lot and ask the Lord to protect us. At night

91

sleeping out in the jungle was terrible. With the monsoon rains and bugs, you couldn't really get any sleep.

"One night they sent a squad of us with one machine gun out to find a whole battalion. This one guy had been smoking marijuana and sucking up cocaine, but he was one of the best guys I've ever seen out there. My squad leader went out and smacked it out of his mouth. He told him that he'd better never get high while on patrol again.

"Since I was a new guy there, I got all the bad jobs. They gave me a machete, and I would have to cut the elephant grass, jump on it and get it so the others could get over it. For thirteen hours a day I would do this. One time we were pinned down for three days and had to call in artillery fire to help us out.

"We would walk by trenches filled with bodies. The rats were so big; they were as big as a cat over here. I had one run across me one night in a foxhole because we forgot to leave some food outside for them. We learned to live with it, and most of the time they wouldn't bother us if we left enough food for them.

"The helicopters would land to pack off the bodies, and the elephant grass would catch on fire. Our Marine bodies had been lying out there for two weeks or more in the hot sun. One guy would grab a couple of arms, and another guy would pick up two feet, and that's all that would be left to put in the body bag: two arms and two ankles. You'd have to wear rubber gloves to eat for two weeks.

"I became friends with a two-year-old child. The war wasn't his fault, and it wasn't his mother's fault. We would help them whenever we could by bringing food to them. The VC had taken all they had. I couldn't stand to see those little kids suffer so we went in fairly regularly and brought food over for them to eat. This little boy would sit on my lap, and I'd give him goodies to eat. The guy that worked with us took a can of ham and threw it and hit this kid right between the eyes. It enraged me, and I picked him up and threw him in some wire, rifle and all. I went down and checked the little boy out, and he was all right. For the most part, the group that I was with tried to help the villagers and the kids. We realized that it wasn't their fault.

"For me to keep my sanity, I tried not to realize the whole scope of what was going on. Every person you walked by was a possible death trap. That's how life was over there. We didn't know the enemy. We could be talking to them in the daylight hours, and find them out trying to kill us at night. If that wasn't enough, you had snakes, spiders, pits and bugs to attend to.

"We were in an area that we'd been in for quite awhile, and I guess I

Larry Hiller

Larry and Diane Hiller (September 19, 1987)

got careless. We had befriended the villagers, and they found out when we'd be going out, and they set a booby trap. I was just a couple of miles from the company when I stepped on a land mine. I was careful, but I guess I wasn't too careful after all.

"They wanted to amputate my leg. I told them that I wanted to keep my leg no matter what. A doctor came to me and said, 'If you think Vietnam was tough, this will be the toughest fight of your life. It's going to take everything you've got to fight this thing. But if you help me, I'll do what I can to save your leg.' I couldn't think of anything else, and I did keep the leg. They told me I would never walk on it, but I did. Then they said I'd never run, but I did. They said I'd have to use a cane, but I didn't. By the time I'd finished, they stopped telling me what I wasn't supposed to do. I was determined that the land mine was not going to get me down.

"When I came back to the States, I found that people called us baby killers, spit at us, mocked us and told us we were stupid and foolish. I thought I was doing what I was told to do. It was our country that turned their backs on us. I'm not ashamed that I shed my blood for my country, and I'd go again if I had to.

From Vietnam to Hell

"I had flashbacks, cold sweats, nightmares and the whole works. I'm not as bad as some people, but I still suffer from PTSD. For a long time, I had to stay off whiskey because I would act like I was back in the jungle again. I wasn't an alcoholic, but I just couldn't drink without getting into fights.

"It was only by God's grace that I was able to be healed of a lot of scars left from being over there. One of the biggest ways He helped me was through introducing me to my wife. When I met Diane, she had a deep impact on my life. The Lord used her to penetrate certain areas of my life where no one had ever been allowed before. Her family was very close, and her father was a decorated man from World War II, and he liked me. They accepted me into the family right away. My wife is just a good woman, and she's probably my best friend in this whole world. Her family helped me and I could talk to them about Vietnam. I could adjust to family life again by watching them live. My wife taught me how to love all over again. After we'd been married for four years, we met the Lord. That really turned me around, and I came to know a really good man, David Knight, who is pastor of the church we joined in Washington.

"A few weeks ago I was sitting in the living room and my daughter caught me totally off guard. I was very tired and uptight, and I went to sleep in the chair. My daughter came in and bent over to give me a kiss, and I knocked her across the room. She started backing out the door, and I apologized to her. It's things like this that I hope will leave once and for all.

"It's been a long period of adjustment for me, and I know I'm still adjusting in many ways. The Lord has had to strip me of a lot of pride, violence, and a spirit of demanding that things be the way I thought they should be. These were survival traits in Vietnam, but they were things the Lord had to adjust in me.

"I'm excited about what God is doing in the country of Vietnam, and what He's doing in healing our vets. Jesus is the only answer, and He's making himself known in some powerful ways right now."

Mike Harris

U.S. Navy

"Spring came early in nineteen sixty-six, and my future plans were reeling through my head. Having been an above average student and relatively successful in sports, I had my future unfolding in front of me. I would soon follow my brother to Oregon State University and fulfill my dream of becoming a teacher and coach. Vietnam was a funny little name that I would see once in a while on the front page of our local newspaper. Little did I know to what magnitude that little country would affect my entire life. I had plans of getting my education, marrying, and having children to share my life with. It was the natural American dream.

"My problems all started that evening when Jerry offered me a drink. Through high school I had retained my image by not indulging in any artificial substances even though many of my friends chose to do so. I was proud of the fact that I had not given in. Then that one evening at college I relented. From there it was a few beers here and a few there. I couldn't concentrate on my studies and began to be defeated academically. When my draft notice came, I was half scared and half relieved. I was scared of what my future might hold, relieved that I would be freed from the intensity of college life.

"I had a while to make a choice, and it seemed like Vietnam took on a whole new focus. It began to gain meaning instead of just being printed matter. The reality was becoming clear. There was a war on, and young men were dying there. What should I do? My father and grandfather had served their country gallantly. Was I to do the same? I was confused because it seemed only a handful were serving their country, and the rest were carefree and ignorant that any war was even being waged in that faraway country called Vietnam.

"I weighed my options and decided to join the Navy for four years instead of being drafted for two. I felt that my chances were better in the Navy. The word was that most of those that were drafted into the Army were shipped off to Vietnam in the infantry. As I recollect, that was definitely the case. So, feeling I had made the right choice, I boldly stood in front of the San Diego International Airport ready to do my time. As the Marine drill sergeant barked orders in my face, I accepted the challenge to serve my country in the best capacity that I could. I was unaware at that time that it would be on the front lines of battle in the rivers of Vietnam.

"Boot camp was a real challenge to me. I had grown up in the country and knew the woods well. Several years of scouting had honed my skills. Then participation in athletics helped me mature even more. I was little for a fullback, but I soon became a threat to our opposition. I was always first string and attained a trophy for most valuable player three out of four years in high school. My senior year, I led our league in touchdowns and carried the ball more than anyone else in the district. I was the 'workhorse' and proud of it. This would carry over into my naval training and eventually cause me to volunteer for service in Vietnam. I became the right guide in my company during boot camp and then moved to squad leader. It definitely had its benefits. I very seldom stood watch like the others and was never assigned to KP. As we progressed through our training, I saw others fall by the wayside. They could not handle the stress and rigors of constantly being harassed. I enjoyed it! I could handle anything that they could give me. Others were the same, and we bonded together in little groups because we knew that we could take it. I even remember a couple of individuals attempting suicide. This seemed like foolishness to me. In retrospect, I truly feel sorry for them. They had come out of situations that were much worse than mine, and I had no empathy for them at all.

"The excitement welled within each of us as the chief began to read out our job placements. After a battery of tests, each individual was placed according to how the Navy thought he was best qualified. As my name came up, 'Radioman' came off his lips. Radioman? That sounded ok. I knew instantly why I had been selected. My grandfather was a ham radio operator, and I had sat in his radio shack many nights, listening to him send and receive morse code and I was always in awe. Between him and my father, they had taught my brother and me how to send and receive it also..That knowledge had helped us in scouts and would soon assist me in 'Radioman A School.'

"During this time Freddy and Bob had become my best friends. We drank and ran around together, basking in the San Diego sun at Ocean Beach during our time off and learning all about transmitters and receivers while at school. Bob was naturally smart while Freddy and I were a bit slower. About that time our instructor put out an urgent plea for volunteers

Mike Harris

Michael Harris

to go to Vietnam. Radiomen, so we were told, were in great demand. Without hesitation, my arm shot up into the air. With my eyes riveted on my instructor, I hadn't noticed that Freddy had raised his, too.

In a couple of weeks, the orders were processed, and it was time to find out our fate. Freddy and Bob's last names started with B so their orders came first, "Mobile Riverine Force, Republic of Vietnam." Freddy sat quietly while Bob groaned out loud. My mind was racing. I was going to war! How was I going to react? What would my parents think? I could hear my heart, along with Bob's groans, beating in my ears. It must have been a feeling similar to being told you had a terminal illness. We were to find out later that it *was* like a terminal disease to some individuals, they never returned alive.

"I began to grow up fast. Every word that was spoken by my future instructors was absorbed to its fullest because it might save my life. As the training grew more intense, the reality of war did also. We were taught to use hand grenades, .45s, M-16s, 20MM cannons, 40MM cannons, shotguns, and even BB guns for quick kill methods. We went without food and were harassed in mock prisoner of war camps. The closer our time for departure came, the more fatalistic we became. We fought amongst ourselves at the club for something to do. Freddy was from Mississippi. One evening after a few beers, he began to taunt some blacks at the club. He stood five foot tall but was built very well for his size. I always told him that was why I hung around him. The club closed, and when we stepped outside, the black guys were waiting for us. Four of them grabbed Bob and me, and held us back while a couple of others proceeded to beat Freddy. I can still hear him laughing. He knew that he was getting what he deserved. The next day he had a couple of bandages on his head and some bruises, but we all knew that he reaped what he had sown.

"The big day had finally come. As we boarded the big Braniff jet, I had mixed emotions. I remember thinking that I might never return. We were only eighteen years old. Why were we going to war? We had barely learned how to drive and couldn't legally vote or drink. Now we were headed for a foreign country to fight for a people we didn't even know. Outwardly I tried to act tough, but inwardly my mind was screaming.

"As we flew into Honolulu, we were so rowdy that the captain told us that our flight would have to be held up if we didn't settle down. A deafening roar came over the fuselage, and we taunted him back with, 'What are you going to do, send us to Vietnam?' We felt indispensable until our plane banked to make its final descent to Tan Son Nhut Airbase in Saigon. Then an eerie silence came over the soldiers. We saw the bomb craters and began to relent to the reality of our situation. As the cabin door opened, we knew we were there. The hot humid air rushed in like a sauna. Strange odors couldn't escape our noses. Even today, these odors come back at times. My senses are still titillated by diesel, urine, helicopters, and many other things. The direction of my life was changing fast. There were times to be sober and times to party. We began to recognize them and take full advantage of them. At first it seemed like 'Charlie' could be around every corner. Later we knew when danger was near. We still had that invincible attitude. In a short while, it would be softened.

"The day my boat arrived on the merchant ship was a proud day. It was to be home to seven of us for the next year. We all painted cherries on the back of them because it was the thing to do. When you received a direct rocket hit, you would paint a crack through your cherry. We commissioned River Assault Squadron 15 and had fifty boats on line in a short time. Of those fifty, forty-eight took at least one rocket during our year. Some took almost two dozen. My boat, T-152-1, never got to paint a crack through her cherry. It was remarkable. We had rockets go over, through, and beside us in the water, but not a one hit its mark. I witnessed many boats take direct hits, and Freddy's boat was hit twice with rockets, and he was wounded both times. Bob's was the only other boat that couldn't paint a crack through its cherry. I heard him groan more than once though.

"We had our slow times when we would be in the larger part of the Mekong. Compared to combat, it was dull, and we would circle the larger ships for twenty-four hours at a time to keep divers and mines away from them. Then it was back to the A.O., and I came to enjoy, in a strange way, returning to the intensity of the rivers. It was more dangerous, but the time seemed to pass so much faster. We would be on edge with our adrenaline flowing strong for days on end. You never knew when Charlie would strike. When he did, it was pandemonium! We were taught to shoot short bursts on our machine guns. In a firefight you shot as fast as you could. I screamed and yelled during these encounters and was surprised how I hung in there and poured out the lead. It was our only defense. It was hot enough without having a roaring .50 caliber machine gun with an almost transparent glowing red barrel spitting out death in front of you. After each encounter it took us a long time to come down from the intensity of the battle. Invariably we would have wounded or killed amongst us. Often we would have to turn around and go back through the ambush in order to get back to safe territory. It was worse knowing that we were going to get it again.

"I only saw the enemy on two different occasions aside from the prisoners that our troops would capture. One time I caught a glimpse of a group of VC shooting their machine guns at our Medivac chopper. It got so intense that the pilot decided to pull out. One of the Army medics grabbed the skid as the bird left the boat. I watched as he hung on for dear life. The pilot evidently didn't know he was there and made a quick maneuver. As the chopper banked, the medic's grip was lost and he flailed as he fell into the jungle. I often feel that he is still listed as one of our MIAs.

From Vietnam to Hell

"My boat and T-152-10 were cut out of the squadron and sent to Rach Gia to operate in 'Charlie Canal' with some PBRs. As I look back, it's a wonder any of us made it out of there. The PBRs were so fast that they decided that we should transit to our place of debarkation approximately an hour ahead of them. We would trade nights with Tango 10 and transit alone down those VC infested rivers. There was no gunship for cover for us. We just made eight knots down that river.

"It was our turn out one evening, and we ended up running aground and bent a shaft. We limped back to the Vietnamese Naval Base and started preparing for repairs. Tango 10 had punctured their fuel tank and wanted us to go back out, but we couldn't in the condition that we were in, so they patched the hole and went out. Later that evening we heard our radio erupt with rifle and rocket fire. They were being hit hard and someone on a PBR had to board them and steer them out of the ambush. Charlie had hit them with four rockets. One hit Barry in the chest and splattered him everywhere. Three more hit in the swain flat, and gun turrets wounded everyone else on board. We couldn't believe the carnage the next morning. All we could do was to put the pieces that were left of Barry into a 20MM can and dump it over the side. The larger parts went home to his parents. That was December twenty-seventh, nineteen sixty-eight. His Christmas packages continued to come in, and all we could do was open them and share what he would have enjoyed. All this happened during a cease fire.

"As we sat drinking beer while waiting for our plane to fly us to Saigon to depart, a rocket landed in the midst of a bunch of Army guys waiting for their convoy to arrive. They were troops of the 9th Infantry and were the first to depart from the war zone under Nixon's Vietnamization Program. Three returned in coffins. We were only one hundred meters away, and it could have been us that were killed.

"Next, we flew to Saigon and were told to stay in a specific Navy building. Freddy and I went down to a Vietnamese bar and spent the night. We were wondering if we would ever get out of that place. After waiting in a long line of jets to take off the next morning, we finally departed for the "world" with cheers and tears. There were cheers for having survived and tears for those who hadn't. It was too early for the heavy drug scene in Vietnam, but most of us left as hardcore alcoholics. We had made up for the tough times by drinking ourselves into oblivion when we had the chance. It would affect most of us for years.

"I remember landing at Travis AFB outside of San Francisco so happy to be back on American soil. I jumped off the lower step of the ramp and knelt down and kissed the earth. It was a joyous moment, but it didn't last long. We were warned about the protesters. We were shocked. They kept

Mike Harris

us away from them and bussed us out the side gate so we wouldn't have to confront them. All I wanted to do was get on the plane to go home. When I arrived home, everyone was glad to see me, but there was something strange, even with my parents. They didn't really want to talk about what had happened to me. It was like everyone wanted me to start over right there and forget what had happened. How could I? It was the most major thing that had happened in my young life. I had just turned twenty-one, and I seemed to be much older. My friends were still in their mode, and to this day I never renewed those relationships. Years later, my mother, whom I dearly love, told me that I might as well have been dead when I returned.

"Since I had joined the Navy for four years, I still had nineteen months to do on Guam at the Naval Communications Station there. Having made E-5, I knew very little about what they had trained me for in radio school. I was awarded medals for valor soon after I arrived and got in serious trouble the next week for giving an obscene gesture to an Air Force general. My attitude was rotten. I hung out with the young guys because I was one of them. Guam gave me the opportunity to drink all the more, and it got me into trouble, but I loved it. I would have nightmares about Vietnam, and the drinking would help. If I passed out, I wouldn't dream.

"Finally I was discharged from active duty. I had saved up five thousand five hundred dollars and was determined to drink it away. My brother was living in California so I stayed there with him and continued to get myself into trouble with my drinking. I moved to Washington State after nine months and did the same. It was as if I were suicidal. I spent every cent I had on booze. Once in a while I would indulge in marijuana or other drugs, but as long as I had my beer I was ok. My life was taking a downward spiral at an accelerating pace. I failed in all of my relationships and despised authority, especially anything to do with the government. Through the years I became more and more isolated. If something went wrong, I would go into a rage, kicking and breaking things. Even in my horrible state, I knew that I needed to get out somehow. My health was failing. I thought I had friends, but most of them were taking money from me. I teamed up with a 'Nam buddy, and we proceeded to try to drink everything in town. My motive was to always get as drunk as I could if I started to drink. Ninety percent of the time I succeeded.

"Finally in nineteen seventy-six I had to do something. I had tried to quit, but it just got worse. I was drinking a lot of wine at the end and would get sick on purpose out of desperation. One day I went around and told everyone that I knew that I was quitting for good. That committed my pride, and I was able to struggle through it. Like a fool, I replaced my drinking with drugs. Marijuana was my mainstay, and at one time I got heavily into prescription diet pills. I had tried LSD and cocaine but fortunately didn't get high like I thought I should. The marijuana use increased, and my health began to fail again. I tried to stop but couldn't. Here I was at thirty-three and failing. Then a strange thing happened to me. I had always vehemently refused to listen to anyone talk about religion. One day, someone asked if I'd like to look into the Bible. Without hesitating, I said yes. It shocked even me! Four days later, while sitting in my kitchen by myself, He spoke and said, 'Flush your drugs down the toilet!' I responded by saying, 'What about Randy? He uses them.' He said, 'He doesn't need them either; flush them down the toilet!' From that day on I never have had a desire for drugs again. He had truly made Himself real to me. Since then, my life has been changing every day. I feel renewed and have a direction again. All hope is not lost. We can rest in Him.

"I had been trying to contact Freddy for many years to no avail. Little did I know that he had been trying to do the same. After a few beers, he would have his wife Connie begin calling around Oregon for me. One day I called the right city. It was nineteen eighty-five, sixteen years after Vietnam. The phone rang and a voice answered a bit reluctantly. I knew it was him. It took a little convincing to let him know that it was me. We both wept while trying to talk to one another. There would be long pauses because neither of us could speak. I was finishing up a job and promised him that I would head to Mississippi right after completion. I did, and we had a grand reunion in June of that year. After spending two weeks there, we both stood in the hot sunshine with tears in our eyes again. He didn't want me to leave, and I didn't want to go. I knew that I had to, though. I didn't know that I would never see him alive again. Six months later he was killed in a single car accident heading home from his local pub after a few beers. To date, over one hundred twenty thousand Vietnam veterans have died of suicide or single car accidents like Freddy's. The statistics are astounding.

"I went back down to help Connie with the funeral and do what I could for his son Jason. While there I kept having protective feelings towards Connie. I would go to bed at night and pray, 'Lord, if these feelings are not of you, then I don't want them.' They continued and during the next few months, Connie and I drew closer via the mail and telephone. One day I asked her to marry me, and she accepted. We have been married for three years now, and I am raising Freddy's son who is almost seventeen. He looks and acts a lot like Freddy when I met him in boot camp. The Lord has been good to us these few years. My life has improved, and we are now working with the ministry that reaches out to Vietnam veterans and their wives.

"It is called Point Man Ministries and at present has over one hundred fifty outposts in various cities and towns throughout this country and other foreign countries. They also have 'homefront' chapters that reach out to the wives of these veterans since they have been so affected by the vet. I am proud to be part of what is happening and delighted in how our Lord has stretched out His loving arms to me.

"When I had been saved about two years, the Lord spoke to me mightily. He said, 'You can deal with multitudes of people!' I was thrilled! But He came right back and said, 'But, you need to deal with yourself first.' That is so true for all of us. If we neglect to deal with ourselves, then we cannot reach out and help others. I still have a long way to go, but I thank Him that I have come this far. For all of you reading this, nothing short of a miracle has happened in my life. I've seen the same happen in many others' lives. All He asks of us is to choose with our will to do His. We have that awesome choice. I hope you think about it and choose to do so. You will NEVER regret it!"

Astrid Ortega, RN

Army Nurse Corps

"Writing about my experiences in Vietnam as a nurse has been difficult. It made me delve into my mind and recall events that were sad and painful for me. Thinking about my experiences brought back flashes of memories, dreams about old friends, nurses who were so close to me that year. Part of the process I went through was to read Lynda Van Devanter's book, *Home Before Morning*. It set my thoughts flying to the reasons I joined the Army Nurses Corps in nineteen sixty-six.

"My parents moved to Providence, Rhode Island from Merida, Yucatan, Mexico, in nineteen forty-nine. My father, a physician, had an internship at Roger Williams Hospital. I grew up around medicine and hospitals, and at the age of fifteen, I decided I wanted to be a nurse. While a student at Rhode Island Hospital in Providence, I heard that one could join the Army Nurse Corps and travel after graduation. So I did just that.

"In September nineteen sixty-six, I drove to Fort Sam Houston, San Antonio, Texas, for basic training. My two best friends from nursing school were with me. It was an exciting, fun-filled eight weeks.

"After training I was stationed at Lettermen Army Hospital, Presidio, San Francisco. I enjoyed my experiences there. Harassment by some of the nurses in charge about dating enlisted men, who were closest to our own ages of twenty-one and twenty-two, was an ongoing torment. All parts of my life, including time off, were closely scrutinized by the Army. It came as a great shock to me when in July of nineteen sixty-seven, I was given orders to ship out to Vietnam. I had not volunteered for that duty, so I was not prepared to leave the safe environment of San Francisco. I had heard of horrors of the Vietnam War from my GI patients, who were all victims of that conflict. I felt I was doing my patriotic duty by being the best nurse I could be at Lettermen.

"On August tenth, nineteen sixty-seven, I reluctantly left Travis Air Force Base and flew for twenty-four hours to 'my great adventure,' as I thought of

Astrid Ortega

it. I landed by commercial airliner in Tan Son Nhut Airport, Saigon, Vietnam. After three days at Long Binh, the powers that be decided where I was to serve my country as a nurse for the next three hundred sixty-five days.

"As luck would have it, I was sent to the 36th Evacuation Hospital in Vung Tau, the in-country 'Rest and Recreation' center for soldiers on leave from their units. Located on the coast of the South China Sea, it was fifty miles south of Saigon, on the mouth of the Saigon River. It had miles of tropical beaches, sea breezes, plentiful sunshine and many wounded GIs to remind us that a war was going on. It had been called the Riviera of the East. The French had built and left many beautiful villas on the shore. The small town of Vung Tau had at least three hundred bars and more than six hundred bar girls who plied their trade on the vacationing GIs. We young, naïve nurses soon learned a great deal about life and venereal diseases.

"The nurses and doctors of the 36th Evac. lived in an old nineteen fifties French hotel, the 'Villa du Bois.' We called it the 'Vung Tau Jail,' as we were often confined to our quarters due to frequent mortar bombings in the area. We actually had very comfortable living arrangements: two nurses to a room with a shower and a small refrigerator. We even had a Vietnamese woman as our maid; Mamasan was paid five dollars a month by four nurses to clean our rooms, do our laundry, and polish our boots. My fellow nurses in Vietnam had it much rougher than I did. Vung Tau was considered the plum assignment and the safest place to be in Vietnam.

"As a 1st lieutenant, I was promoted the month I arrived 'in country.' I was assistant head nurse of a GI post-operative ward. I was responsible for more than forty-four wounded GIs, young men in their late teens. Most of them had leg and arm wounds, frequently double amputees. Some of my patients were Australian and Korean soldiers. One young Australian 'leftenant,' as they were called, had walked on a land mine. He survived. Ian would ask me every day how he was going to tell his bride of six months about his injuries. This fellow had both his legs and his left arm blown away. I could only tell him that she would understand and that the Australian government would help him get artificial limbs. I often felt helpless and angry at the waste of the lives of so many young men. Incredibly enough, we nurses were told not to cry in front of our patients as it would make us appear to be 'weak women.'

"My schedule was heavy — ten to twelve hour days, one day off a week, occasionally two days off in a row. The young lieutenants had to work nights, while the higher ranking Army nurses had the day shifts. They who said rank has its privileges were not kidding. One of my unpleasant memories of Vietnam was the harassment by the 'lifer nurses' about maintaining Army etiquette, such as saluting even if you had your hands full,

From Vietnam to Hell

Astrid Ortega (1967)

wearing your ugly Army baseball cap, and not dating enlisted men. We non-lifers felt it was silly to concern ourselves with such nonsense when we might not be alive tomorrow. We had heard about nurses dying in Vietnam, but it was not a publicized fact. I now know that eight nurses died during this war, and another six thousand two hundred fifty nurses served in Vietnam.

"I did not mind working hard; I learned so much about being a caring, empathetic nurse from the American, Australian, Korean, and Vietnamese soldiers that I had the privilege to know.

"The ward I worked on was made out of a half of a Quonset hut; the bottom was made of wooden siding. There were large screens on the windows to try to keep the majority of the insects out. It let in the red clay dust that covered everything during the dry season. During the rainy season, red mud would ooze over the cement ward floors. My main concern was to keep the GIs comfortable, to give pain medications and debride wounds.

"The last five months of my tour, I took over a ward of Vietnamese women and children who had been injured in the war. A fourteen-year-old girl, Kim, served as my nurse's aide and translator. It was tragic to see a forty-five bed ward full of these displaced people. Each patient was given a Walt Disney character name; we never took the time to learn their Vietnamese names. So my ward was populated with Snow White and the seven Dwarfs, Bambi, Thumper and Dumbo. These patients were cared for by us because their own country's hospitals were full. From the Vietnamese people, I learned the meaning of stoicism in the face of physical and mental pain. Their adaptability to our ways and our GI food astounded me. They asked for very little pain medication and would thank us profusely for anything we did.

"Kim was the last person I saw as I flew out of Vung Tau by helicopter on August fifteenth, nineteen sixty-eight on my never-to-be-forgotten DEROS (Date of Expected Return from Overseas). I had counted those days until my return to the real world.

"My return home was a combination of elation and confusion. After being treated like a queen by the gallant men in Vietnam, I soon learned I was a nobody to the military people at the Oakland Military Base where I was discharged from the Army. No ceremony, just, 'Here is your discharge pay, and goodbye.' I was shocked to hear people in San Francisco say, 'You were a fool to go to Vietnam.' I soon learned not to tell anyone I was a veteran, except for my two nursing school buddies who picked me up in Oakland. They were supportive and did not ask a lot of questions.

"I was lucky enough to have two dear nursing school classmates who had served in Tuy Hoa. When I returned, I lived in New Jersey, and they lived in New York. We would get together on weekends and talk over our experiences and what we planned for our lives in the future. They were my support group for the next ten months. I later moved to Los Angeles with two of my ex–Army nurse friends in nineteen sixty-nine. I didn't experience the worst kind of trauma because I had someone to verbalize with who had been in Vietnam also.

"That is the thing about nurses; they had nurse friends that they could tell how they felt and talk to, but the men didn't have that; I had a close family and could talk to them about my experiences. In fact, when I came back to the US, I decided to visit my family in Mexico. I just vacationed and got my head back together. I think all the talking helped me get it out of my system. I did think about and dream sometimes of Vietnam and the horrors that we all had to witness, but it wasn't as much as some of the nurses did.

"My brother went to Vietnam even though I begged him not to, and he has a different perspective about the Vietnam War and the people over there. He was in the infantry and was hurt twice, and now he can't stand to even see Vietnamese people. He doesn't talk about it very much, and one time we went to the Wall in Washington, DC. I went through a counseling process about eight years ago with a woman named Rose Sandecki. She was the head of the Veterans Counseling Center and has done a lot of work with the nurses and their traumas. She has a degree in psychiatric counseling and runs groups for women. It was a helpful group, and I learned a lot from that.

"The coming home process took a long time. I now lecture on Vietnamese culture and health beliefs to other nurses. Maybe it is to appease the guilt I feel for not having learned more about the Vietnamese people while I was there. Maybe it is to make up to them for calling them Walt Disney character names. I work with these people, and that helped me to get rid of my guilt.

"As a nurse we took care of the Vietnam people also, so we didn't have the animosity that the soldiers did who were out there fighting them. For the most part, the nurses liked the Vietnamese people, and we saw them as human beings. They were just a different culture.

"I am troubled by the political naïveté of some nurses. Many nurses are moved by my slides of Vietnam. They tell me that they never understood until now why the Vietnamese are refugees in our country. If I can impart some small cultural awareness, then what I went through for one year in my young life will have been worth it."

John

U.S. Marine Corps

"My name is John and I'd prefer not to use my last name. I don't trust many people anymore, but the story of Vietnam needs to be told. I've been through hell since the Vietnam War. My life was ruined and no one cared. I'm outraged at the whole thing. I went to war at the age of nineteen to fight for this country, and when I came home they were upset with me. I feel like a time bomb, that I could go to jail at any time because I might do something stupid. I can't handle authority or someone telling me what to do. Right now I'm out in the woods by myself.

"When I first went to Vietnam, I was scared like all the others. We were young and knew we were going to war to be killed, wounded or whatever, and it was scary. When we landed in the country, we didn't know what to do. The people who had been there awhile didn't want anything to do with us because we didn't know anything, and they felt their lives would be jeopardized. The jungle itself was beautiful, green, blue vegetation, and the water in the mountain streams was crystal clear. I was a rifleman during the Tet Offensive in nineteen sixty-eight. I stayed basically in the jungle, so my contact was mostly with the NVA soldiers.

"The NVA were trained soldiers, and we would fight face to face. They usually outnumbered us. The United States would tell the people back home how many we had killed. In reality they were hitting us hard, and that's where the Agent Orange came in. They decided that they would kill the foliage so we could see the NVA. They sprayed chemicals over the jungles, and it killed the foliage, but it also sprayed on the men and later caused cancer.

"We never got much sleep in the jungles. Even the days we didn't see the NVA, at least three men would be shot in the head by snipers. You never knew if it would be you that day or if you were one of the lucky ones. I was eating lunch one day with my buddy, and we were talking about his girl back in the States. A round hit him in the head, and I had his brains in my lunch and all over me. He never felt a thing, but I did. I've never gotten over it and I don't think I ever will.

"They would tell us that we had to stay up at night, that this was the night the NVA would come in and we needed to be ready. Can you imagine thinking that all night long? We were all so tired, but we didn't sleep. Nothing happened that night. I became so unfeeling at nineteen years old that, after a fight, I would pack up the wounded and send them off. I would pick up the dead and throw them in bags, and then we'd eat lunch. We'd sit down and eat lunch. We had to be hard; we were Marines and you couldn't let anyone see that it bothered you. You had to be a man and take it. I opened up my lima beans and ate them. Do you know why we ate the lima beans after a fight? We hated them but after seeing the death and destruction, you didn't taste them. That's why we ate them at that time.

"I had been in country about six weeks when we had to go out on patrol one night. I had dysentery and asked the sergeant if I could miss that one patrol. I was sick and didn't think I could make it, or be of help to anyone else. He said in no uncertain terms that I was going if I was dying. So I went down the trail with them. I was so sick, and it was uncomfortable. I wasn't trying to get out of going into the bush, I was just plain sick. My temperature was going up as the day wore on. The medic said that I should go back, that I was too sick to go on, but the sergeant said I would go on or die. They were not going to send a chopper in to take me out. I drank all of my water because I was so hot and feverish. Then I traded my fruit cocktail for a couple of swigs of water from the guy in front of me. I didn't have any more valuables on me, so I didn't get any more water. These guys didn't want to have anything to do with me because I was new in the country. They thought I couldn't take it, getting sick and all. We didn't make contact all day with the enemy. We reached our destination and got some water to drink. It was Thanksgiving Day, and they were cooking turkey and instant potatoes. I wanted to eat so badly, but I was so sick that I couldn't. The sergeant came over and asked me if I was going to eat. I told him that I was too sick, so he just left me there and went down to eat. Finally I was put on a chopper and sent to the hospital. I woke up and the nurses were cleaning me. I smelled so bad and had sores all over my body. Two weeks later, I was back in the bush again.

One day on patrol three of our men disappeared. We didn't know what had happened to them until the second day. We came upon their bodies on the trail. The NVA had defaced them, cut off their penises and stuck them in their mouths. We were uptight now. We were scared because they might do this to us if they got a chance.

"I remember it was Christmas, and I felt tears in my eyes. I said to myself

John

that I was in some serious trouble. My nerves were getting bad, guys were dying like flies all around me, and it was kill or be killed. We were fighting in their backyards, and we stood out like sore thumbs, ready to be ambushed. They would use snakes to get us, put them about face height so we'd walk into them. They called them the five step snake. You couldn't go five steps after being bitten before you died. They had all kinds of booby traps. Sometimes they used poison gas, but the greatest fear we had was to be a POW.

"When I came back to the United States, I couldn't believe the people would be mad at us. We thought we were heroes for laying our lives down for our country. We were warriors and had fought our war. They called me 'baby killer' and 'rapist,' and I couldn't understand it. I hadn't done any of that over there, but the people here didn't understand the war. All they could do was place the blame.

I couldn't hold on to a job because of the PTSD. At first I thought it was normal for me to have hallucinations and dreams about Vietnam. I thought the flashbacks and the tiredness were normal, too, but they weren't. It was a symptom of post-traumatic stress disorder. I would take sleeping pills to get some sleep at night. The pills kept me drugged, but the VA wanted me to take them. I needed outside help since the VA wasn't doing anything but giving me sleeping pills. I went to a psychiatrist who treated me for the PTSD. I tried to get money from the government because of the PTSD, but the government refused. I think the veterans have a real problem and should be helped for their safety as well as for the safety of other people. We went to war to fight for our country. They send us out here with no money and some of us are unable to work because of the mental and physical stresses. If you can't work and support your family and it's because you fought for the government, then they should help us. They should have deprogrammed us as soon as we reached the US. I think it would have helped a lot of us if they had had some sort of programs for us.

"For years after Vietnam, I lived out in the woods. I would wash in the stream, eat cold food, and go to the bathroom in the woods. Finally I got a little heater and would heat some of the canned food that I ate. I was getting modern then.

"I've been diagnosed as having severe PTSD. I went to the veterans' centers and they helped. I couldn't hold a job for very long, and I couldn't sleep. I began to smoke a little marijuana; then I needed something to wake me up. It was a merry-go-round. I keep on having nightmares and flashbacks about Vietnam. I get into fights all the time because I can't stand somebody telling me what to do. I find myself on the edge of life all the time. Vietnam did that to me.

111

From Vietnam to Hell

"I used to sleep with a gun all the time until one night I was having a flashback and found myself shooting at some trees. I decided not to take a chance on that happening again. My wife could have come walking down the path and been killed.

"I don't believe we belonged in Vietnam. They told us in training we were going over there because they didn't want the Vietnamese over here fighting on our backdoor and raping our women. They said it was necessary to go over and fight the war. I didn't see any necessity in it. We went over there with the good intentions of cleaning up these bad guys and coming home as heroes. That was a joke. The other wars were necessary, but not this one. My child isn't going to war for this country.

I can remember the happiest day in Vietnam. We were on the jet on our way back home, so high that the Vietnamese couldn't fire at us and that was a very happy feeling. We knew that now the only way we were going to die was if the jet were to crash. We were almost home with all our arms and legs. We weren't going home in a basket; we were going home in one piece. Little did we know, most of us were eaten up with Agent Orange, PTSD and traumas. We thought we were all set; we were going back. We got home and found out differently.

"I've driven eighteen wheelers all over the country but can't seem to last very long at any one place. Vietnam haunts me today; I hear the groans of the dying. Everyone yells out to God when they know they're dying, and I used to wonder if I would do the same.

"A man can't kill another man and be the same as he was when he was a child. You can cover it up and pretend, and try to forget it, but it never goes away. It poisons you, robs you, and changes you from what you once were. What I once was I can never be again because I fought for my country. A child went to war, and a crazy man came home. I don't know of any other way to put it."

Craig McLaren

U.S. Army

"I was born in West Palm Beach, Florida, on April twenty-first, nineteen fifty. Both my father and grandfather as well as many uncles were WWII vets, and the military always seemed like the ideal career.

"I was a good student in school and lettered in band, swimming and track. As a teenager I was taken to see some recruiters a couple of times, so immediately upon graduation from high school, I enlisted in the Army. After a year of Army schools, where I received more training than the regular Infantry or Marines get, I was sent to Vietnam.

"I volunteered Airborne, Rangers and Recon and was sent into combat with the famous 173rd Airborne Brigade. I was stationed in 2nd Corps Area, and my unit accounted for more enemy kills than most divisions. Divisions are eight to ten times larger than brigades. We patrolled areas from the South China Sea to the central highlands and to the Cambodian border. I was decorated and under fire on a regular basis and wounded in action.

"I was injured twice and once at the Evacuation team in Qui Nhon where I was sent to 12th United States Air Force Dispensary in Phu Cat to be hospitalized. I was admitted for, among other injuries, an acute anxiety reaction and given many barbituates. I was released after three weeks with my back, ribs, and leg taped up. I was sent back to my unit with a pocketful of Seconal. Because of some mix-up with the 67th Evac. team's paperwork, I got an Article 15 for AWOL when I got back to my landing zone. I was still patched up, and they sent me back into the bush.

"I was WIA and MIA, and received thirteen personal decorations including three Bronze Stars, a Purple Heart, air medals, Arcom, VSM, VCM, CIB, etc. for bravery and valor from the US government and four combat and civil action awards from the South Representatives of Vietnam government

"After coming back home to Tampa, I felt guilty, confused and dirty.

113

I would take three or four showers a day. I was increasingly using drugs and alcohol which was upsetting my parents, and I got no help from the government.

"I enrolled in junior college at St. Petersburg, Florida, a month after coming back. I found I couldn't stay in my classes or concentrate on my subjects, primarily because of my drug and alcohol use. Even though I was above average in intelligence, I was placed on academic probation for four quarters before I got married. For a short period during college, I tried to hold down a parttime job, but could not. I didn't respect civilian employers.

"After one more semester of college at another campus (I transferred to be away from the drug scene, but I brought that to the new campus with me), I quit and turned to fulltime employment. Since I had not had any kind of training, I started construction work. Being outdoors and working with my hands helped to keep my mind occupied. As different projects on Florida's Gulf Coast finished, I found I wasn't making enough to support my wife and me.

"I then decided that my wife and I would join the Army together. We went to enlist and both passed our mental and physical tests. Soon they sent her to camp, but even though I had been going to summer camp and risking my life jumping out of airplanes at Fort Bragg, North Carolina, they said I had to get a waiver to reenlist because I had an unfavorable code number. My father and I finally went to see Congressman S. Gibbons, and it took many months of paperwork to get the waiver.

"I dealt drugs and made many trips back and forth visiting my wife at WAC training. We settled in Huntsville, Alabama, where we chose our station of duty, so I wouldn't be in a combat arms. Again, after several different construction jobs, the Army finally wrote that I would be accepted, but only for a combat field because of my prior specialties.

"I began getting high quite a bit and started experiencing blackouts. The doctors had given me drugs for the constant headaches that I suffered from. The day that I went to the Armed Forces entrance station I was escorted off the post by the MPs for drunk and disorderly conduct. The second time I went back they signed me up.

"After two schools, both combat, I came home on leave. My attitude was harsh and my wife and I quarreled and fought. I was being sent to a crack battalion combat team, the 509th Airborne Infantry in Europe. This would cause a long separation for us. I stayed high all through my last Stateside leave. I was doing everything according to the book while on duty in Europe, but off duty I began smoking hashish and drinking whiskey even more than I had been doing.

Craig McLaren

"We were always on alerts, and I jumped into Germany, Italy, and Turkey many times. I was one of the few men ever to be selected as a NATO exchange soldier to go to the honored German Paracommando School. There in Merzig, West Germany, I received the Bronze Jump Wings Award to wear on my American uniform with my other medals and badges.

"Once back in the States I was arrested and went to trial in November nineteen seventy-five. I did not tell my lawyer anything about my mental problems, even though in Italy I had been commanded to attend drug and alcohol programs and, the Army sent me to a psychologist who prescribed medication.

"On May thirteen, nineteen seventy-six after a long and highly publicized trial, I was convicted and given a life sentence for first degree murder. My lawyer did not call any witnesses for me. The Army finally discharged me in nineteen seventy-nine, with an 'under other than honorable conditions' discharge, effectively depriving me of my benefits for school, even though my first discharge for six years was honorable, both active and Reserves. I was not just a soldier; I was a trained killer and was combat tested by Uncle Sam. I never received debriefing or counseling after coming back from the war. If I still need psychiatric help, then there must be some way I can get it. I have seen a psychiatrist here in prison and, after ten minutes, he gave me Thorazine, but not counseling.

"I am not responsible. I am not even sure if I did this crime or not. If I did it, it's not my fault. There was no knowledge of PTSD at the time of my trial. I should be treated not confined. I never wanted to hurt anyone, and if it happened, it wasn't me, not the real me.

"Veterans in prisons during the early years after the war were completely forgotten by the nation they had served so well. Men who had fought so bravely and bled for their country, earning awards, medals, and decorations, were doubly convicted by the press and media who labeled all Vietnam vets as 'drug addicts and baby killers.' This, of course, influenced juries across the country to convict a Vietnam veteran quicker and for the judges and prosecutors to give them longer sentences than the average criminal. This was a mockery of justice as the Vietnam vets were usually first time offenders, but they routinely got longer sentences than the multiple offenders. It was unfair and unjust. Once in prison, the vets had no recourse to help them, no understanding, and there was no knowledge of PTSD.

"The majority of veterans sent to prisons for violent crimes were combat vets. Only one out of every eight soldiers in Vietnam were combat. This shows that the U.S. government and our military high command failed to counsel these returning warriors. They had been trained to fight and kill. They had been trained to act and react quickly and violently and to survive.

From Vietnam to Hell

Then they were sent home from the fields of death without the slightest debriefing or reintegration programming. I, like many others, got so depressed I withdrew from life and seriously contemplated suicide as the way out. At a recent general membership meeting of Chapter 190 of the Vietnam Veterans of America, Inc., I read aloud an article called 'The Marketing of Perversion' by Mark Masters, from *New Dimensions* magazine [January 1989]. Over one hundred Vietnam veterans and associates gave a big round of applause. We, as Vietnam veterans, well know of the perversion of the national press. We've experienced the terrible effect, as a class, of the media packaging of the 'illusions and perceptions' of the masses. We served our nation honorably, in what may have been an ill-conceived foreign war, yet we faithfully answered our nation's call to duty. We were as brave, loyal, and dedicated as any other generation's civilian soldiers. Yet we were vilified, defamed, and dishonored by the press.

"The media marketed dozens of falsehoods and lies. The illusion was created in papers, magazines, and nightly news that we, the true young patriots, knowing no more of global politics than our fathers who fought in Asia and Europe, were 'crazed killers and drug addicts.' This is untrue.

"The facts are plain. First the media worked to destroy Americans' faith in their government and their respect for our flag, giving more respectful television coverage to the flag burners and only short bites and thirty-second spots on dead U.S. servicemen or wounded Vietnamese civilians. They never showed our successes against overwhelming odds, nor mentioned that ninety percent of all civilian casualties in South Vietnam were a direct result of Viet Cong and North Vietnamese Army actions.

"The media packaged and sold the anti-war movement. But I'm not saying that anti-war was wrong, rather, that America's young men and young women who served were made the villains, and that we were cast falsely as the perpetrators of atrocities and genocide. The media turned the nation against the warriors, not just the war.

"No one can value peace as much as one who has seen the horrors of war. No one can respect the value of freedom as much as one who has fought for it. These are not merely gold-plated clichés, but truths. Those who can be labeled as the 'warmongers' and 'hawks' are those who never faced battle.

"Things can change, by enlightened and free thinking individuals working to right the wrongs and correct the misperceptions. I offer the attitude reversal witnessed in the last few years toward our Vietnam veterans. We had to build our own memorials and give our own welcome home parades. And it has been but a small minority, less than ten percent, who have been active in this process. But we've made an extremely big difference.

116

Craig McLaren

"You can be a force for enlightment, not merely by promoting rational thought and morality, but by pointing out the illusions each and every time you see them. You can write to the editors, networks, and publishers to rebut and correct. Speak up at school board and community meetings. Attend local meetings and make your views known.

"Remember the forces of darkness can't stand the light. Let's turn the light back on in America."

In 1984 Craig began in earnest to put his talents and energies to work to be of service to Alabama's incarcerated veterans. He then founded Alabama's first Chartered Veterans' Prison Group, Vietnam Veterans of America, Patriotic Americans Commission, Veterans of the Vietnam War, B.R.A.V.O., National Incarcerated Veterans Network, Point Man Ministries, and Home Free Committee. He created and edits America's first *National Incarcerated Veterans' Newsletter*, *The Eagle Speaks* and now also published *The Eagle Update*. He is the author of *Incense & Jade*, *The Smell of Cordite*, *The Strength of Steel* and *Blood on the Bamboo*.

McLaren's V.V.A. Chapter 190 is the largest and most active Incarcerated Veterans' Organization in America. He has been recognized by many national veterans organizations for his wide range of accomplishments. He was named National Volunteer by V.W.M.P. in February of 1988.

His goal is to access full veterans' rights and benefits for America's incarcerated armed forces veterans. He praises God for each and everything he does, feeling that His work is his mission. His deep and sincere dedication to the cause of equal rights and justice for all incarcerated vets is because of his true Christian faith. He asks for the prayers of all his brothers and sisters, Christians and veterans.

Sam Grashio

U.S. Army

"I was a platoon leader in I Corps, South Vietnam, nineteen seventy thru seventy-one. Throughout most of my boyhood, I dreamed and played games in which I envisioned myself in a jungle environment fighting against an Asian foe. The reason was that my father had been an Army Air Corps fighter pilot during the Second World War. He was taken as a POW in the Philippines by the Japanese when Bataan fell. After a year of surviving brutal atrocities, the march of death, starvation, sickness, disease, filth, and other inhumane treatment by his captors, my father and nine other American servicemen escaped. Eventually nine of the ten brave men reached freedom, my father included.

"As a young boy, I was fascinated by my father's recounts of those jungle wartime experiences to his fellow Air Force aviators. Because of my father's influence I grew up believing it was a privilege to be born an American. That privilege was earned when a man did service for his country. I was taught that integrity was a virtue to be valued. I therefore accepted my Army orders to report for duty in South Vietnam. In fact, I volunteered.

"I arrived in South Vietnam in late August nineteen seventy. Like most men that are preparing to face combat for their first time, I had spent many agonizing hours trying to realistically visualize combat, and I tried to predict how I would react once real bullets were flying at me. It did not take me long to find out.

"My imagination had been working double-time since the previous afternoon when I had been told I would be joining my unit in the 'bush' that following morning. I know every man that has faced combat remembers what the first day was like. I was noticeably nervous and anxious, more from fear of the unknown than a fear of injury or death. I knew that until I had experienced the real thing, I could only guess and wonder at the reality of combat.

118

Sam Grashio

"The exhilarating thirty minute helicopter ride from the 11th Brigade rear area at Duc Pho to the front lines seemed to add to my rapidly rising anxieties. C Company, 3/1, 11th Brigade was loggered in a company perimeter. I clumsily jumped from the skids of the hovering re-supply helicopter to the dried-up rice paddy about five feet below.

"I no sooner hit the ground and was trying to orient myself when this high-pitched, ear-piercing scream came screeching out of the blue skies. It was closely followed by two earth-shaking explosions up in the high ground at the base of those steep, green, gem-like mountains. Rocks, branches, stumps, and dirt burped out of the attack area while the ground around me rumbled, twisted and rolled from the impact of those five hundred pound bombs. An ear-shattering sonic-boom rapidly followed the sleek American attack jet aircraft that zoomed so close overhead. I suddenly realized that I was the only grunt standing; the other one hundred-odd grubby, dirty, unshaven and foul-smelling men in the company were all prone on the ground. I quickly dived behind a small mound of dirt just as AK-47 rounds snapped, popped and crackled when they passed about a foot above my head.

"Two enemy RPGs passed overhead and slammed into the dry rice paddy fifty meters behind me. The ground jumped and rumbled again. My heart was banging against my chest. I was confused, disoriented, and did not have a clue as to what I should be doing. I realized that then was not the time to try and find out just what to do. I hugged the ground tighter. I became aware of the burning, intense sun, the sticky-hot humidity and a certain mustiness that almost oozed from the tropical floor. The combination of the three made the air so thick that it almost choked me.

"Another jet swooped in, dropped its ordinance and flashed by, climbing rapidly into the bright sun. Then artillery rounds began to hammer into the smoke-streaked low hills where the enemy was dug in. For a second or two, it was deathly quiet. Suddenly the wild cacophony of M-16s being fired again filled the air with deafening effects. The NVA on the high ground had ducked into their bunkers, caves, and trenches, or else they had slipped further up into the dense jungle mountains. There were no longer any incoming rounds. I lay there behind my steel pot (helmet) with my nose almost buried in the ground. The artillery rounds began shifting up the mountain and into the adjoining draws and ridges. The rounds were impacting onto all possible escape routes that the NVA might have tried to utilize.

"The grunts of C Company began to come out of their foxholes and fighting positions. I became aware of radio transmissions coming from C Company's CP (command post). I picked myself up from the ground and sheepishly made my way towards the crackling and hissing company radios.

119

From Vietnam to Hell

"There, huddled on the ground, was a young blond-haired captain. He looked me over ever so quickly and went immediately back to transmitting on the radios. Then he paused, looked back at me and said, 'Lieutenant, you have got Second Platoon. They are preparing to move out and secure that high ground. Pritchard is your platoon sergeant. He will fill you in on what we are up against. You will find Second Platoon's positions about one hundred meters out, by that tree line,' the captain pointed and then went back to transmitting on the radios. He glanced back over at me. 'Move out now lieutenant. We will talk later,' he ordered.

"As I made my way towards Second Platoon's positions, I passed various members of the company. What a motley crew this was. They all had combat-hardened eyes, with piercing stares that looked through a man.

"After a brief introduction to the Second Platoon sergeant and squad leaders, we immediately moved towards our objective. In less than three hundred meters we ran across a single strand of communication wire. I did not realize the implications of such a discovery. Unbeknownst to me, only large concentrations of NVA were in the habit of stringing commo wire between command posts. (We were in the middle of an NVA battalion. The commo wire indicated that they were here to stay.)

"The platoon became more cautious and began to spread out so as to minimize casualties in the event that we were hit. We moved no more than another thirty to forty meters when the air was filled with automatic weapon and machine gun fire. I was down on the ground under my steel pot. My heart was, for the second time that morning, banging violently against my chest. Rounds began to snap in the air directly over my head. I was trying to figure out from which direction we were taking fire. But it wasn't until I saw one of the squad leaders point to muzzle flashes that I had a clue where the NVA ambush was located.

"Within moments, friendly artillery rounds were impacting where once enemy muzzles flashed. Dirt, bark, and vegetation coughed and spit out of the mountainside. The platoon was ordered to pull back so that brigade could bring some big stuff to be dropped on the enemy base camp. Second Platoon was moved to a position some five hundred meters to the southwest and set up as a blocking force along the banks where a mountain stream fed into a wide river. The remainder of that morning and into the evening those enemy positions were hammered by a continuous stream of aircraft and artillery. Even the Navy got in the act when one of the battleships stationed in the South China Sea fired its big guns onto the enemy targets.

"Early the next morning Second Platoon was ordered back into the

Sam Grashio

NVA base camp. I thought it hardly likely any living thing could have survived the bombardment of the previous night. I soon realized that only I had such an optimistic view. The others knew only too well the tenacity of our enemies.

"We crossed the stream next to our blocking positions and began to maneuver towards the high ground. PFC Butler, the Iceman, was on point. His total concentration was on the ground immediately to his front. Suddenly he shouldered his M-16 and pointed his weapon to his front. Like the legs on a centipede, the column of men behind him reacted to the point man's actions. The platoon was down, every other man pointing his weapon in opposite directions.

"I was the fourth man in the column, and the Iceman glanced quickly back to me, the platoon leader, for what must have been approval. In that moment that he looked back, I saw what must have alerted him. A light green and khaki uniformed NVA soldier came crouching out of a hedgerow and took aim on the Iceman. I shouldered my M-16 and emptied a full magazine into the man.

"In that instant before I fired my weapon, the NVA rifleman and I had eye contact. In that fraction of a second, a very strange phenomenon occurred. My life's experiences flashed before me, and a gnawing question presented itself. Why are this man and I trying to kill one another? I saw fear in that man's eyes just as he must have seen the same fear in mine. I realized that he no more wanted to die than I did. He was a pawn just as I, the difference being only in each of our political beliefs. The underlying factor was that I was in his backyard, a trespasser. In my mind's eye, I saw my well-aimed rounds find their mark and tear the life out of that NVA soldier. It did so in blood-splattered slow motion, almost as if I were again dreaming.

"It wasn't until I attempted to slam a fresh full magazine into my M-16 that I became aware of the burning painful sensation in my right arm. Almost simultaneously, a well-aimed RPG exploded about ten meters to my front. The impact and concussion blew me about five feet into the air. I lay there dazed for a moment or two when suddenly one the grenadiers threw his body over mine to protect me.

"I was not prepared for that pure act of bravery that the seventeen-year-old grenadier exhibited. Dirt, rocks, branches, debris, and red hot shrapnel was blowing all around me, but that courageous young man's body was protecting his leader from any further injury.

"I lay there stunned for a few moments. There was a loud ringing in my ears, and my right arm began to ache unrelentingly. Doc Zanzie began to administer first aid. Doc informed me that my wound would buy me some safe time in the rear. It took a moment for it to sink in that I was being Medivaced back to the safety of an Army hospital.

"I must have fainted because the next thing that I remember was being hoisted on the Medivac helicopter and flying away from the smoldering earth below. The jets resumed their bomb runs, and I could see Cobra gunships hovering nearby, awaiting their turn to get back into the action.

"The morphine was giving me a high I had never experienced before. The lush green jungle passing under me reminded me of a sea of marshmallows that some Irishmen must have colored green for Saint Patrick's Day. Everything seemed so ridiculous and meaningless. The past two days flashed before me. I kept seeing the NVA soldier's eyes, the one I had killed earlier that morning. I again remembered looking into those eyes, only what seemed like moments earlier, but actually it had been hours before, and watching him watch me. That man had wanted to live. He was dead. I was alive.

"The Dust Off (Red Cross) helicopter landed at the 23rd Medical Evacuation Hospital, Chu Lai. I was carried by stretcher and put on a litter that was pushed down some hallway. There I awaited my turn to be examined and operated on by a physician. The hallway was cluttered with men like me who were awaiting their turns for a doctor's attention. More litters kept coming in, and it was obvious to me that at least that day 'Charlie' was inflicting some hurt on the US Army.

"I must have dozed off again, but was rudely awaken by the screams of pain of some poor grunt that was strapped to his litter a few feet from mine. Nurses and orderlies were working frantically on him, shooting him up with various injections and connecting IVs to his arms. The sheets covering his abdomen were covered with a crimson splotch that kept growing larger as he lay there. I overheard one of the nurses mention 'gutshot.' I had heard that a gutshot wound was one of the most painful. The screaming of that patient attested to that. The man's moans and screams were making me very uncomfortable and irritable. Why wasn't someone helping him?

"He moaned to himself, 'Someone help me . . . please help me, . . . God help me . . . it hurts too much. . . .' God must have heard him because that was the last thing that GI ever said. He was dead. The orderly came and wheeled his litter to another part of the hospital. A nurse came by and gave me another shot, and the next thing I remember, I awoke on an operating table with three surgeons going over me. Then I was wheeled to a recovery room where I promptly fell asleep.

"I had trouble sleeping the remainder of that night. Every time I closed my eyes I would flash on either the eyes of that dead NVA soldier or on the

Sam Grashio

faces of various men of Second Platoon. Mostly I flashed on those eyes. I kept wondering about him and his life before this day. I kept questioning the necessity of this war. I wondered if I really could justify it enough to lead men into it again. It was not just fear that was making me question the right or wrong of what I was doing; I had learned to rationalize the fear. It was more the morality of my involvement. How could I be effective leading men in a cause I wasn't sure I understood or even believed? How could I put my life and the lives of the men of Second Platoon on the line for a cause I could not justify? How could I even ask myself these questions when I was right in the middle of the involvement and unable to control my own situation? Those were my thoughts as I lay on that hospital bed in that very foreign country eighteen years ago. It no longer mattered to me if we won or lost; it only mattered that we survived.

"After many hours of throwing this conflict around in my head, I finally closed my eyes and listened to the waves from the South China Sea roll in and out on the near shore. I also heard some form of Asian music from an unknown and nonexistent source, as if that mysterious Asian country was playing a victory song for my enlightenment . . . survival.

"During the duration of my time, I found that life in the Chu Lai-based Medivac hospital was luxurious compared to life in the bush. Even though I had had no more than three days experience as a grunt, it did not take long to realize that combat in Vietnam was comprised of a multitude of hardships for those brave men doing the actual fighting.

"Yet there existed a genuine comradeship that closely paralleled love between men that shared constant life-threatening dangers, unforgettable physical hardships and common foxholes. Ironically, relationships formed during the heat of battle, on steamy jungle mountain trails, in humid rice paddies, or along numerous murky brown riverways. Little did any of us know that Vietnam-based relationships would be the dye from which all future relationships would be cast. Unfortunately the majority of us would never experience such pure love again when we returned to the world we so intensely missed.

"I was discharged from the 23rd Medivac Hospital and promptly hitched a ride to the Eleventh Brigade's rear. It was a well-fortified area, ringed with four men. There were concrete bunkers every thirty meters. There must have been almost a hundred bunkers. Within the bunkerline existed all the amenities of a stateside military installation, and I felt very safe within its confines. There were hustling GIs everywhere.

"I had already bled for the cause, and my bleeding would forever make my war experiences intensely emotional and very personal. I realized that unless you actually got the blood, brains, and guts all over you, unless you did the killing and remember the cries of pain, the screams of terror, and experienced the silence of death, the horror of Vietnam could not be appreciated.

"I knew now was the time to return to take command of Second Platoon. My right arm had healed enough so that I could accurately fire my M-16 and maneuver satisfactorily in the jungle. The wound was no longer a consideration. I had worked the arm extensively the past three weeks in the hopes of rehabilitating it. I thought that it was now recovered sufficiently for me to return to the bush, so I requested permission to return to command Second Platoon. This time permission was granted.

"It was with some apprehension that I returned to take command of Second Platoon. Overcoming the fear to again lead in combat was something that actually gave me the inner strength I needed to return to the bush. A warrior must come to terms with fear every time he leaves the safety and security of a rear area to face the constant danger of a combat environment.

"What survival now came down to as far as I was concerned was simply to use all the resources available to kill the enemy before he killed me. That had always been the idea, but now I understood firsthand the price one paid when dead. Death now really had a meaning for me. Death was not a game played by a young boy growing up. Death was real. Death was cold, silent, noncaring, nonfeeling, like a rock, timeless nothing. Death was a phenomenon that lived in the bush. That was a fact I knew all too well.

"In the summer of nineteen seventy-one, when I returned home from Vietnam, I remember feeling out of place, as if I did not belong. I was uncomfortable and noticeably nervous when the plane touched down in my hometown, Spokane, Washington. I was apprehensive about meeting my parents and relatives at the airport. Ironically, however, I had spent three hundred sixty-five days longing for this very moment. I had anticipated the day and even dreamed about its arrival. Now that it had arrived and I was safe in the 'world,' I felt I wanted to return to the 'bush'. I felt especially concerned about the welfare of the men with whom I had served and those I had led, the men from Second Platoon and Charlie Company. What I really hoped for was that the war would soon end and that all the US servicemen would come home with as little loss of life as possible.

"When I returned from my tour of duty, it was obvious to most Americans that the war was not being fought with winning in mind. The majority of the returning Vietnam vets knew firsthand that policies and subsequent decisions backing those policies rendered the military effort all but useless. I was angry with the system that allowed Vietnam to become the disaster that it had become. The fact that US involvement had not been directed towards winning was impossible for me to accept. I was ashamed that the US government signed the 'Peace with Honor' that we did with North Vietnam. I was disgraced that we knowingly left the South Vietnamese in an impossible situation. Even more appalling, however, were the MIA issues. The question 'Did the US government turn its back on the MIAs that were being held against their wills?' haunted me.

"My first night in my room in my parents' home was a night of many emotions. I was elated to be alive and physically healthy, but at the same time I felt surges of survival-guilt. Knowing that I had made it home in no way eliminated my memories of the relationships and the experiences shared with those men close to me, those I fought with and even those I fought against. Nor did it relieve the empathy I held for the suffering and hardship I knew that many human beings were being exposed to in Southeast Asia.

"I remember trying to borrow around six hundred dollars from a local bank to buy an older model 356 Porsche. I had three thousand of my own money and needed a small loan for the balance. When the bank in question realized I was a veteran recently returned from Vietnam, they denied me the loan.

"I went to work for a construction company and found that the physical exercise of working on a heavy construction site offered me all the opportunity necessary to vent my frustrations and anger. I was a whirlwind of energy blasting through the tasks of the day. I did not realize it then, but my system was still programmed to work on survival instincts utilizing energies I had honed while in the bush. I still had the ability to call on those instincts at will. The problem was that I could not slow myself down. I had so much energy and unexplainable anxieties that the combination confused me. I thought that everything and everybody had changed. Little did I realize that only I had changed. Values and behavior that I once readily accepted had all been altered through my combat experiences. Exposure to combat and the acceptance that I could be killed at any given minute instilled an intense desire to live within me. I wanted to enjoy life to its fullest. I wanted to live and feel every minute of every day. As I looked around and observed people, I could not help but question their motives and direction. I could not understand how the people back in the 'world' could continue to live their lives and not be concerned for those servicemen still serving the American government interests in Southeast Asia. I was appalled that the condition and height of one's lawn was of more concern to Americans than the outcome of American involvement in South Vietnam.

"I no longer was the naïve product of American society. Vietnam had given me an education in reality. I had learned the real meaning of death. I

From Vietnam to Hell

knew what death smelled like, and it had a smell that turned the stomach. I knew what death looked like; it looked waxed-gray. I knew what death felt like; it felt cold and rigid. I knew what death did to the mouth; it made it thick and dry. And I knew what death sounded like; its silence was deafening.

"In Vietnam I had become addicted to the thrill of combat. The excitement and challenge of living on the edge had become a part of me. I, therefore, found life out of the combat zone to be very boring. When the boredom combined with my extremely high level of energy, I found myself in a most undesirable situation. I had no way of knowing or understanding what had changed me. But I had changed. I tried to return to the life I left behind before entering the Army, but I did not fit in because I no longer had the same values. But I did not understand any of this in the summer of nineteen seventy-one.

"I began trying to come to terms with what I had experienced in Vietnam. However, it seemed that every time I would attempt to have an intimate conversation that dealt with Vietnam, I would be turned off by whomever I was having the discussion. Because I was so intensely wrapped up in that Vietnam experience, I must have scared people away, but I did not perceive it that way back then. To me, most Americans just did not care unless they had been there personally.

"I was proud of how the men in my command conducted themselves in the most dangerous and diverse combat situations. We were not baby killers, nor did we treat the Vietnamese population with disrespect. Thankfully, most of my combat was against a uniformed enemy, the NVA. Therefore, for the most part, I knew the enemy; I did not have to distinguish him from the local populace as those fighting the black pajama–clad VC were forced to do. I wanted to share my war experiences but found that too few were willing to really listen. It was not long before I found myself trying to put Vietnam totally behind me. The only possible way for me to do that was to try and forget that it had existed.

"I tried to forget, but every single day I would find my mind reliving those memories of Vietnam. I could not get Vietnam out of my mind. Sounds, smells, and memories constantly took me back to that mystic, war-torn country. I would find myself reliving specific 'fire-fights' and ambushes. I would vividly remember numerous NDPs (night defensive perimeters) that we had occupied. I would remember every detail about that location; terrain, climatic conditions, stars and moon positions. I would go through any number of Vietnam experiences in a similar intense manner.

"I was confused because I did not understand why I was experiencing flashbacks to Vietnam periodically throughout the day. I wanted to be in Vietnam, but at the same time, I was so grateful to be home and alive. I would think about various Vietnamese that I had befriended and wondered what the future held for them. I doubted it would be an enviable situation. I felt guilty because I was home while other Americans were still fighting and dying. Loyal South Vietnamese were being abandoned to the mercy of the enemy.

"As I watched the drama of Vietnam unravel via the news media, I became more and more disgusted and angry with the end results. I believed that my government lacked integrity, and those beliefs were reinforced when Nixon was impeached for unethical practices. I lost all confidence in the American system. I began rebelling against the system in my own way.

"I looked to find a means to challenge myself. I needed to satisfy the craving for excitement. I decided to go to Mexico and put all those talents the Army taught me to good use. I began walking marijuana across the hilly area at the border near Nogales, Mexico, south of Tucson, Arizona. I picked a route that only mountain lions, rattlesnakes, and lizards would inhabit. Along with a team of two other Vietnam vets, we soon perfected the route and walked the grueling twenty-mile trek twice monthly at night.

"It became a thrilling and exciting event, not unlike leaving an LZ (landing zone) and beginning a mission in combat. It had all the ingredients of a combat zone because there were the Mexicans to deal with, (they could go either way, for or against you, it varied from night to night. Sometimes the Mexicans would try to ambush us to get back and resell the pot), and there were the authorities on both sides of the border with which to contend.

"Not any less important, there was the physical hardship of backpacking seventy-five pounds across the Pena Blanca area of Mexico and Arizona for a distance of twenty miles or more. The trek had to be accomplished at night before dawn. It allowed me to put those energy and survival instincts to what I rationalized was a good use. What it really gave me was a sense of satisfaction because all I was doing was venting my pent-up anger from Vietnam.

"At the time I easily rationalized an acceptance for my behavior. Marijuana was not considered a dangerous drug. In fact, it was generally accepted by American society as harmless. The opportunity was always there to smuggle harder drugs, such as cocaine, speed and downers, but those I thought were in a more dangerous category, so I avoided any involvement with them.

"I devoted myself to the time-consuming and energy-burning endeavors of smuggling and transporting marijuana from Mexico to the Northwest. It was always a small operation because we walked the contraband between the US and Mexican borders and the mules (those men transporting the drug across) were all usually combat Vietnam veterans. I knew that they could easily get the job done. We had learned how to project a positive end to a difficult situation. We did so every time we successfully completed a mission when we were back in the bush, therefore we knew the attitude necessary to realize a positive result for our smuggling mis-adventures. Yet to a man, it was the satisfaction of knowing we just snubbed our nose at the American system that gave us our most prized rewards.

"The challenge of remaining successful in that illegal endeavor drove me to continue to test my luck and abilities against the authorities again and again. I made myself believe that so long as I remained rational, I would be able to handle any situation that might arise. After all, I had survived the combat zone, so why wouldn't I survive the relative safety of the arid Southwest desert? At least that entire countryside was not at war.

"About this same time I remember dreaming the same dream two or three times a week. In it I am leading a patrol along a jungle mountain trail. As the patrol continues to maneuver, I become aware that there are enemy soldiers whispering all around me; they are waiting for the most opportune moment to spring an ambush. The enemy soldiers mass together and start chasing the patrol through the jungle. Eventually I am alone and trapped in a box canyon. The enemy closes in as I turn to face what I know is certain death. At that point I wake up. Sometimes I hear a spine-chilling, bone-wrenching scream. It startles me to realize that I am the one screaming, and I am drenched in a cold sweat. What surprises me is that it is always the same dream with the same results.

"I knew that something was wrong or at least something had changed about me, but I was never capable of putting my finger on it nor of fully understanding how, why, or what had changed. I continued to live one step ahead of the authorities. It was a personal vendetta that I was playing out between myself and the system. I was rebelling.

"By nineteen eighty I was beginning to notice certain behavioral trends in me that were not at all desirable. I would become angry over absolutely nothing and would vent my anger either verbally or physically on whoever or whatever was nearby. My father finally insisted that I make an appointment with the local VA Outreach Program. It was there that I was given literature that dealt with PTSD and its characteristics.

"I was interviewed by a counselor and, after a few more appointments, I was directed to the VA hospital. After a series of tests and interviews, it was concluded that I was suffering from PTSD. I was experiencing many of the characteristics common to PTSD: depression, emotional numbing, headaches, a constant change of jobs and addresses, solitude, an inability to trust 'the system,' flashbacks, dreams, and nightmares of Vietnam, and an overall inability to accept the realities of life.

"I had been escaping from reality through the use of drugs in an attempt to numb my senses to all that was going on around me. I stayed under the influence of drugs for the better part of fifteen years. I became an addict. I had changed my drug of preference to cocaine and was hooked on crack or base cocaine. That is the form of cocaine that is smoked in a pipe. It is deathly addictive. It was not long before I had alienated myself from all family except for those with whom I did drugs.

"In nineteen eighty-three I began reading everything that dealth with Vietnam. I wanted to understand as much about what actually happened as possible. I know that those changes I experienced were also experienced by every American that had seen combat. It became obvious to me that many combat Vietnam veterans exhibited similar behaviors and almost all of them were angry most of the time.

"It was not until nineteen eighty-five when my daughter, Alexandria, was born that I began to try and come to grips with what I had turned myself into, an addict. I committed myself to a VA drug rehabilitation center in August nineteen eighty-six. Six months later, I had relapsed and was back using drugs at a more reckless rate than before. In November of nineteen eighty-seven, I again entered a VA drug rehab program and am clean today.

"In nineteen eighty-eight I was introduced to Point Man Ministries and have become an active member of the local chapter in Spokane, Washington."

Arthur Brown

U.S. Army

"My name is Arthur Brown, and I'm forty-five years old. I entered the United States Army in March of sixty-two at the age of seventeen. Prior to going to Vietnam, I spent two separate one-year tours of duty in Korea, and for some reason I fell in love with the Orient and the Oriental people. During my second tour of duty in Korea, I met and fell in love with a Korean woman, and we were married in January of sixty-six. So, in a way when I got to Vietnam, it was a lot like going back to Korea, the land, the smell, and the people.

"I went to Vietnam in July of sixty-seven. When I first arrived in-country, it was hard to believe that it was a war zone. It seemed so quiet and peaceful, but that was only to last a few days while I was being processed in-country.

"After about my fourth day there, I was assigned to the 11th Armored Cavalry Regiment in Zuan-Loc, Vietnam. After I got off the chopper in our base camp, I realized that I was in a war zone. In a way I felt like I had some advantages over many of the soldiers there. One was the fact that I was twenty-three years old, a sergeant E-5 with six years active duty. I had already spent two years in the Orient, so many of the sights, sounds, and smells were not new to me. I was not an eighteen-year-old kid, straight out of school, or off the streets and shipped to a foreign land.

"My job in the Army was a supply sergeant, but I soon learned that I would be called upon to do many things other than supply, and it didn't help to be assigned to a front line combat unit. After I got engaged in my first battle, I loved something about the war, maybe the feeling of power. It was a high that I had never experienced before in my life. I remember when I first arrived at my unit in July. At that time there was no such thing as a war atrocity, and we were allowed to do anything to a Vietnam national that we wanted. What cleared us of any wrong doings is that we would declare him or her as a suspected VC.

Arthur Brown

Arthur Brown (1967)

"I remember my first confirmed kill. Things were getting boring back at the base camp, being the S-4 supply sergeant. I didn't get to go out on all the operations, and only got to go out on the major ones where we would be out for a period of time until we would need to be resupplied. When things got boring at the base camp, I would volunteer to take a squad out on ambush patrol. There were usually thirteen men in the squad: one officer, usually a 2nd lieutenant because they were expendable, myself and the NCO, one medic, two radio operators, two M-60 machine gun operators, two M-79 grenadiers, and four riflemen.

"The way we worked the ambush patrols is that we would go out in the afternoon and recon the general area that we were going to operate in that night. We would ride out on the sides on tanks or on top of an armored personnel carrier, whichever was available to take us out. We would scout the area to see if it looked like there had been any activity recently. We would return back to our base camp, and wait until just before dark, then load back up on the tracked vehicles and go back out, dropping off the vehicles, and moving into the area by foot so that it was dark before we got into position to set up the ambush.

"During this time of the war (1967), we had a kill zone. Anything that moved from seven at night until seven in the morning was killed. We were not required to challenge anyone moving around. They weren't supposed to be out there, and they knew it, and we knew it, so that meant that they were VC or VC supporters, and that meant anything that moved, we killed.

"On the night of my first kill, it was early morning and things had been quiet all night. At the break of dawn, one of the men noticed a man riding

131

a bicycle and stopping and getting off, and looking around as though he had lost something. He would ride up the road a little farther, and then get off and begin to look around again. About one hundred meters down the hill from our ambush sight was a small hut. As he was approaching the house, from the left to the right, I instructed my two M-60 operators that I was going to work my way down the hill to behind the house. If the suspect went past the house, I was going to open up with a burst of machine gun fire. I positioned one man in the front, and one to the rear, and told them to watch for me to give them the signal when it was time to fire.

"When the man emerged on the other side of the house, and it was obvious that he did not live there, I gave the hand signal to fire, but nothing happened. I continued to give the hand signal, not realizing that they had frozen up on me. I was a good thirty meters from the road, too far away to start chasing him since he was on a bike. I decided that I would try to stop him myself by shooting him with the .45 I had with me. I had left my M-16 up on the hill with my men because I had to work my way down the hill on my belly to keep from being seen by the suspect or anybody else that he may have been scouting for.

"I aimed the pistol at him and shot. The first bullet landed in front of him. He dropped his bicycle and started to run for the tree line across the road. I then emptied my clip of six more rounds at him; one of the shots brought him down. I waited a few minutes to see if he was going to get up and start running again, but he didn't.

"I walked over to him and saw that two of my shots had hit him, one in the leg, and the other in the chest. I never imagined what a bullet could do to a human body, and it almost made me sick, but my enthusiasm outweighed my sick feeling. Right then and there I knew it would never bother me to take another human life. From then on I lived the rest of my tour of duty for one thing, and that was to obtain that high again which I got to do seven more times before leaving Vietnam.

"I also learned that the abundance of alcohol and drugs helped sustain me for the biggest part of the tour. I tried to stay high or drunk just about every day that I was in base camp. One thing that I can say is that the biggest part of the men in our outfit never went out in the field high on drugs. Somehow they realized that the drugs messed with your thinking and reaction, so for the most part the drinking and drugs were done back at base camp.

"Probably the worst part of the war that I saw was the Tet offensive of nineteen sixty-eight. We were assigned to secure the Cholon district of Saigon. Seeing people, especially the children, that had been burned to death by napalm was the most horrible sight. But like I have stated before, I could get past the horrors by the use of drugs and alcohol.

Arthur Brown

"When I returned to the United States (at that time my home was in Hawaii), I had some mixed emotions. I was returning from a war of killing Oriental people, and I was married to one. Even though I loved my wife, the mother of our son, I never could treat her the same way that I had before I went to Vietnam. I always found a reason to physically abuse her.

"Although I never got started back on drugs, I slowly became an alcoholic, and after nine years of abusing her, she divorced me. The sad part is that she never did anything to deserve the way I treated her, other than being born with slanted eyes. Of course I can look back now and realize that the problem was with me and not her. It is many years too late now to change what has happened. We have both remarried and have little contact with each other.

"I personally feel that the United States started out with honorable intentions in Vietnam, but somehow it became a political battle, and our objective was lost. I only hope that if we are ever involved in another war, we are allowed to win.

"It's too bad that a person can't erase his past, like rewinding a VCR film and starting over again. There are things that many of us would change. I experienced the dreams, the flashbacks that are associated with PTSD because of my time in Vietnam. I would see those children who had died or had been burned over and over and it bothered me. I thought it wouldn't, but it did.

"As one of the most powerful nations on earth, along with China and Russia, we are now starting to work with each other and getting along with each other. We should do away with our nuclear armament and such programs as Star Wars. Just think if these three most powerful nations on earth did away with such programs and put the trillions of dollars onto other programs. There would be no homeless or children starving to death in the Third World nations. Who knows? Maybe our grandchildren will live to see it.

"At times, I feel that what I experienced in Vietnam has helped contribute to my coming to prison. But then on the other hand, I have to accept the responsibility and be accountable for the actions that brought me here. Otherwise I will be setting myself up to come back.

"One thing I have learned from my life after Vietnam is that drugs and alcohol do not get rid of your problems. They just delay dealing with them in a rational manner, or land you in prison, or dead."

133

Index

Index

136